New Daylight

Edited by **Sally Welch**   January–April 2018

D1322962

The Bible Reading Fellowship
15 The Chambers, Vineyard
Abingdon OX14 3FE
brf.org.uk

The Bible Reading Fellowship (BRF) is a Registered Charity (233280)

ISBN 978 0 85746 597 9

This edition © The Bible Reading Fellowship 2017
Cover image and illustration on page 139 © Thinkstock

Distributed in Australia by:
MediaCom Education Inc, PO Box 610, Unley, SA 5061
Tel: 1 800 811 311 | admin@mediacom.org.au

Distributed in New Zealand by:
Scripture Union Wholesale, PO Box 760, Wellington
Tel: 04 385 0421 | suwholesale@clear.net.nz

Acknowledgements
The New Revised Standard Version of the Bible, Anglicised Edition, copyright © 1989, 1995 by the Division of Christian Education of the National Council of the Churches of Christ in the USA. Used by permission. All rights reserved.

The Holy Bible, New International Version, Anglicised edition, copyright © 1979, 1984, 2011 by Biblica. Used by permission of Hodder & Stoughton Publishers, an Hachette UK company. All rights reserved. 'NIV' is a registered trademark of Biblica. UK trademark number 1448790.

Extracts from the Authorised Version of the Bible (The King James Bible), the rights in which are vested in the Crown, are reproduced by permission of the Crown's Patentee, Cambridge University Press.

Printed by Gutenberg Press, Tarxien, Malta

Suggestions for using *New Daylight*

Find a regular time and place, if possible, where you can read and pray undisturbed. Before you begin, take time to be still and perhaps use the BRF Prayer on page 6. Then read the Bible passage slowly (try reading it aloud if you find it over-familiar), followed by the comment. You can also use *New Daylight* for group study and discussion, if you prefer.

The prayer or point for reflection can be a starting point for your own meditation and prayer. Many people like to keep a journal to record their thoughts about a Bible passage and items for prayer. In *New Daylight* we also note the Sundays and some special festivals from the Church calendar, to keep in step with the Christian year.

New Daylight and the Bible

New Daylight contributors use a range of Bible versions, and you will find a list of the versions used opposite. You are welcome to use your own preferred version alongside the passage printed in the notes. This can be particularly helpful if the Bible text has been abridged.

New Daylight affirms that the whole of the Bible is God's revelation to us, and we should read, reflect on and learn from every part of both Old and New Testaments. Usually the printed comment presents a straightforward 'thought for the day', but sometimes it may also raise questions rather than simply providing answers, as we wrestle with some of the more difficult passages of Scripture.

New Daylight is also available in a deluxe edition (larger format). Visit your local Christian bookshop or contact the BRF office, who can also give details about a cassette version for the visually impaired. For a Braille edition, contact St John's Guild, Sovereign House, 12–14 Warwick Street, Coventry CV5 6ET.

Comment on *New Daylight*

To send feedback, please email **enquiries@brf.org.uk** or write to BRF at the address shown opposite. You can also tweet to **@brfonline** using the hashtag **#brfconnect**.

Writers in this issue

Ian Adams is a poet, writer, photographer and priest. He is the author of *Cave Refectory Road*, *Running Over Rocks* and *Unfurling* (all Canterbury Press). He is the Church Mission Society's Spirituality Adviser and is a Fresh Expressions Associate.

Amy Boucher Pye is the author of *The Living Cross* (BRF, 2016) and the award-winning *Finding Myself in Britain* (Authentic Media, 2015). She enjoys running the Woman Alive book club and speaking at churches. She blogs at amyboucherpye.com.

Rachel Boulding, who died of cancer in April 2017, was Deputy Editor of the *Church Times*, and the author of *Facing Death* (BRF, 2017) and *Companions on the Bethlehem Road* (BRF, 2012).

Liz Hoare is an ordained Anglican priest and teaches spiritual formation at Wycliffe Hall, Oxford. Her interests lie in the history and literature of Christian spirituality and their connections with today's world.

Andrew John is the Bishop of Bangor and has served there for nine years. He has spent all his ministry in the Church in Wales. Apart from being a bishop, he occasionally attempts marathons (Snowdonia being a favourite) and enjoys time with his now grown-up children.

David Runcorn is Director of Ordinands and Warden of Readers in the Diocese of Gloucester. He is the author of a number of books including *Spirituality* (SPCK, 2011) and *Dust and Glory* (BRF, 2015).

Naomi Starkey is a curate in the Church in Wales, working in Welsh and English across six rural churches. She previously worked as a BRF commissioning editor from 1997 to 2015 and has written a number of books for BRF including *The Recovery of Hope* (2016) and *The Recovery of Joy* (2017).

John Twisleton is Rector of Horsted Keynes in Sussex and has served as priest, theological college principal and diocesan missioner. He writes on prayer and apologetics, broadcasts on Premier Radio and is author of *Experiencing Christ's Love* (BRF, 2017).

Veronica Zundel is an Oxford graduate, writer and columnist. She lives with her husband and son in north London. Her most recent book is *Everything I Know about God, I've Learned from Being a Parent* (BRF, 2013).

Sally Welch writes…

The beginning of a new year can be a challenging period. After the colour and activity of Christmas, the days can seem gloomier and damper than ever; the nights are long and cold; and we are in danger of falling prey to the ailments of the season. Opportunities for fun are limited, perhaps, by the need to tighten our belts after a period of indulgence and it can seem a long time indeed until the first signs of spring arrive. But even in these shaded times, there are reasons for optimism. Resolutions can be made, new patterns created, new habits begun. Seeds of growth can be planted in our hearts and souls which, if carefully tended, can bring forth a spiritual fruit to benefit us all.

To help you with this time of preparation and beginning, there are some wonderful reflections and insights within this issue of *New Daylight*. Naomi Starkey examines the implications of discipleship and the importance of keeping our minds focused on the main thing – 'the testimony about God… Jesus Christ and him crucified' (1 Corinthians 2:1–2). Discipleship is not without its struggles, but there are plenty of people to help us on our journey – John Twisleton is a wonderful travel guide as he helps us to explore the ancient city of Jerusalem and all that it means for the children of God, and Liz Hoare takes us gently through the challenges of those Old Testament prophets Joel and Amos, leading us to greater understanding and appreciation.

We approach Holy Week with Ian Adams' sensitive exploration of some of the most famous passages concerning that time, and finally arrive at Easter to experience the enormous privilege of sharing this festival with Rachel Boulding, who occupies that liminal territory of one who was given less than a year to live at the time of writing her notes. Her reflections, filled with hope and joy and the vital importance of filling each day with a sense of thankfulness, are powerful and moving – a true flowering of the spirit in the midst of apparent darkness; a witness to the eternal love of God.

I thank God for her and for all of you this season.

Sally Ann Welch

The BRF Prayer

Almighty God,
you have taught us that your word is a lamp for our feet
and a light for our path. Help us, and all who prayerfully
read your word, to deepen our fellowship with you
and with each other through your love.
And in so doing may we come to know you more fully,
love you more truly, and follow more faithfully
in the steps of your son Jesus Christ, who lives and reigns
with you and the Holy Spirit, one God for evermore.
Amen

Where it all started: Genesis 1—11

When my parents cleared my aunt's flat in Vienna, as she was going into a care home, they found family tree information she had gathered, some of it going back as far as 1699. Various TV programmes following people tracing their ancestors, and the plethora of online genealogy sites, show our deep desire to know our origins. I've just read that the two questions everyone asks each other in Bali are, 'Where are you going?' and 'Where have you come from?'

The ancient stories in Genesis are an attempt to answer that second question; and often the answer to the second can give us insight into the first. We can read these stories, as many Christians do, as straight history, and attempt to date and coordinate them. Or we can see them as stories about humanity, which are true at all times, and which tell us not so much what happened in the past as what we are still like.

Talking serpents, worldwide floods, people living to nearly 1,000 – what are we to make of these strange tales? The important thing is to take these accounts seriously, though not necessarily to take them literally. The Bible's authority does not always lie in its historical accuracy (though at times this is important, particularly in the Gospels); it lies in its ability to tell the truth about the human condition. The story of Eden, for instance, emphasises not that there was a talking serpent at a particular time, but that humankind is always flawed and inclined to evil and, equally importantly, that this could be different, that we have the potential to be clear reflections of God.

Ultimately there is no such thing as 'straight history', as every historian knows. Each account of events has a particular bias, depending on who the historian thinks are the 'baddies' and who the 'goodies'. Often history is told from the perspective of the winners. The remarkable thing about the Bible is that it tells the story of a people who were often the losers, a vulnerable nation at the mercy of greater powers. These chapters are the background to that story, and they portray a world where, despite human failing and corruption, God is always working for the good of humankind.

VERONICA ZUNDEL

Called to care

Then God said, 'Let us make humankind in our image, according to our likeness... So God created humankind in his image, in the image of God he created them; male and female he created them. God blessed them, and God said to them, 'Be fruitful and multiply, and fill the earth and subdue it; and have dominion over the fish of the sea and over the birds of the air and over every living thing that moves upon the earth'... God saw everything that he had made, and indeed, it was very good.

My late mother once said she enjoyed gardening because she could 'impose her will' on the garden! Is this what the 'dominion' mentioned in these verses is all about – human beings imposing their will on the earth? If so, maybe some environmentalists are right when they say this passage has done untold harm to our threatened planet.

But notice the first thing God says here about the creation of human beings. They are to be 'in our image'. So, what is God's attitude to this world? Does God 'impose his will' on it? It certainly doesn't look like it – God gives us, and the earth, freedom to live and develop. We have the choice of doing good or evil. Our God-given 'dominion' over all nature is not a licence to exploit it, but a duty to care for it, to develop its potential and preserve its balance. In a term popular these days, we are called to 'curate' the earth. Our care of creation is to mirror God's care of it and us.

In the Genesis 1 story of creation, this is the only part that God pronounces not just 'good', but 'very good'. Humanity is not a curse on the earth, but its crowning glory. Note those parallel phrases: 'in his image', 'in the image of God', 'male and female'. Both sexes are equally formed in God's image.

In her book Eat, Pray, Love *(Penguin, 2006), Elizabeth Gilbert says human beings have two basic questions: 'How much do you love me?' and 'Who's in charge?' The creation, and the cross and resurrection, answer both.*

VERONICA ZUNDEL

Bone of my bone

Then the Lord God said, 'It is not good that the man should be alone; I will make him a helper as his partner.' So out of the ground the Lord God formed every animal of the field and every bird of the air, and brought them to the man to see what he would call them… The man gave names to all cattle, and to the birds of the air, and to every animal of the field; but for the man there was not found a helper as his partner. So the Lord God caused a deep sleep to fall upon the man, and he slept; then he took one of his ribs and closed up its place with flesh. And the rib that the Lord God had taken from the man he made into a woman and brought her to the man. Then the man said, 'This at last is bone of my bones and flesh of my flesh; this one shall be called Woman, for out of Man this one was taken.'

Do you understand the opposite sex? I'm not sure I do. It's impossible to tell what's due to nature and what to nurture, but it's clear that we often think and behave differently, even though science can find little difference in our brains. In some ways, every marriage is a cross-cultural marriage!

Yet look at this alternative story of creation (the different name for God suggests this may be by a different writer from Genesis 1). All the emphasis in the man's speech is on the likeness between the sexes, not their difference. The animals cannot be his 'helper', because their capacities are so far below those of the man – they don't even have speech. Yet when the woman appears, the man recognises a counterpart, a creature corresponding to him. Here is someone who can communicate with him, love him back, make up what is missing in his own personality.

The word *ezer* (helper) used here is always used in the Bible of an equal or a superior, most often in the phrase 'God is my helper'. This is a companion, not an assistant.

Where have you seen true communication between the sexes?

VERONICA ZUNDEL

The blame game

They heard the sound of the Lord God walking in the garden at the time of the evening breeze, and the man and his wife hid themselves from the presence of the Lord God among the trees of the garden. But the Lord God called to the man, and said to him, 'Where are you?' He said, 'I heard the sound of you in the garden, and I was afraid, because I was naked; and I hid myself.' He said, 'Who told you that you were naked? Have you eaten from the tree of which I commanded you not to eat?' The man said, 'The woman whom you gave to be with me, she gave me fruit from the tree, and I ate.' Then the Lord God said to the woman, 'What is this that you have done?' The woman said, 'The serpent tricked me, and I ate.'

A few months ago I posted on my Facebook page, 'If at first you don't suc-ceed, blame someone else.' It's a strategy as old as humanity: in families, in politics, even in churches. We never want to admit our own mistakes or wrongdoing. Men blame women (and vice versa), siblings blame each other, incoming governments blame the previous government.

If you read the judgement of God which follows, however, God curses no one but the serpent, who after all initiated the deception/temptation. God's speeches to the man and woman predict the consequences of sin: domination of men over women, a daily struggle to work enough for a living. These are descriptions, not prescriptions; they describe reality in a fallen world, not an eternal decree.

Even in the curse on the serpent, there is a promise of redemption: '[Humanity] will strike your head, and you will strike his heel.' A blow to the head is more destructive than one to the heel: does this suggest human victory, in Jesus, over evil? Certainly the results of the fall are meant to be reversed in the kingdom of God. Humankind here travels from innocent nakedness to shame and the need to 'cover up'. You don't have to take this as literal history to see this as a true picture of our condition.

Pray for situations where there is inequality or oppression.

VERONICA ZUNDEL

The killing field

Now the man knew his wife Eve, and she conceived and bore Cain… Next she bore his brother Abel. Now Abel was a keeper of sheep, and Cain a tiller of the ground. In the course of time Cain brought to the Lord an offering of the fruit of the ground, and Abel for his part brought of the firstlings of his flock, their fat portions. And the Lord had regard for Abel and his offering, but for Cain and his offering he had no regard. So Cain was very angry, and his countenance fell… Cain said to his brother Abel, 'Let us go out to the field.' And when they were in the field, Cain rose up against his brother Abel, and killed him. Then the Lord said to Cain, 'Where is your brother Abel?' He said, 'I do not know; am I my brother's keeper?'

I've recently been diagnosed (for the second time) with cancer, which may require radical surgery. I'm grieving for what may come and, as anger is one of the symptoms of grief, I'm angry with everyone and everything, especially God. But I don't want to get stuck here, or take it out on others (except God – God can take it, having taken worse…)

We are not told, in this mysterious story, why Abel's offering is accepted, while Cain's isn't. It may be a folk story of the early days of agriculture, explaining conflict between herders and settlers. It's more useful for us to focus on Cain's murderous response. Furious with God, he acts out his anger by killing his brother. I don't suppose anyone reading this is a murderer (though it's possible!) but we cannot congratulate ourselves on refraining from killing, for we have likely all had near-murderous thoughts against someone, at some point in our lives. What do we do with them? Instead of expressing them in words, deeds or refusal to care for others, can we instead take them to God, asking for them to be transformed into forgiveness and love?

Cain's question can only be answered with 'Yes'. We are indeed our brother's, and our sister's, keeper, responsible for how we act towards, and think about, others.

'All who hate a brother or sister are murderers…' (1 John 3:15).

VERONICA ZUNDEL

A man's man?

Cain knew his wife, and she conceived and bore Enoch; and he built a city, and named it Enoch after his son Enoch. To Enoch was born Irad; and Irad was the father of Mehujael, and Mehujael the father of Methushael, and Methushael the father of Lamech. Lamech took two wives… Lamech said to his wives: 'Adah and Zillah, hear my voice; you wives of Lamech, listen to what I say: I have killed a man for wounding me, a young man for striking me. If Cain is avenged sevenfold, truly Lamech seventy-sevenfold.'

Personality traits can get handed down through the generations, not only genetically but in 'family culture'. From violent Cain descends violent Lamech, who treats wives as possessions and boasts of his capacity for revenge. This makes more sense of the provision 'an eye for an eye, a tooth for a tooth' (Exodus 21:24) as a limitation of violence, which we need to read as '*only* an eye for an eye' – instead of a Lamech-style escalating vendetta.

It's only recently that I've noticed an extraordinary parallel between this passage and what Jesus says to Peter, when Peter asks how often he should forgive his brother: 'Not seven times, but, I tell you, seventy-seven times' (Matthew 18:22). Surely Jesus is thinking of this statement of Lamech's? In the kingdom of God, unlimited vengeance (seven was considered a number of completeness, so seventy-seven stood for 'as far as you can count') is turned into unlimited forgiveness. Jesus follows his statement with the parable of the unforgiving servant, showing that our ability to forgive is grounded in experiencing God's forgiveness of us.

This is difficult for those of us with a keen sense of justice, who may find it hard to forgive others for deliberate acts of unkindness or neglect. We may also feel, if we have lived a fairly 'respectable' life, that there isn't much God has had to forgive us for. However, I find that the older I get, the more I'm aware of the potential nastiness inside me, and of the divine love that still cares for me despite my failings.

Where in the Bible can we find good models of masculinity?

VERONICA ZUNDEL

Redemption and blessing

Adam knew his wife again, and she bore a son and named him Seth, for she said, 'God has appointed for me another child instead of Abel, because Cain killed him.' To Seth also a son was born. At that time people began to invoke the name of the Lord… When Enoch had lived for sixty-five years, he became the father of Methuselah. Enoch walked with God after the birth of Methuselah for three hundred years, and had other sons and daughters. Thus all the days of Enoch were three hundred and sixty-five years. Enoch walked with God; then he was no more, because God took him.

A lost child can never be replaced, as many parents, including my own, have experienced. Even so, the birth of Seth is a sign of redemption, a new start for the archetypal human family. And the more descendants, the greater blessing. God had, after all, told humankind to 'be fruitful and multiply' (Genesis 1:28). In developing countries, children are still an insurance for old age.

'At that time people began to invoke the name of the Lord.' Why just then? Gratitude for God's gift of children? A wish to restore the relationship lost in Eden? It strikes me that before the fall, when people could (in picture language) hear 'the sound of the Lord God walking in the garden', there was no need to 'invoke the name' – God's presence was an everyday reality. Now in this compromised world, exiled from paradise, God seems far away and people feel they have to start calling, maybe even shouting. And yet Elijah hears God in 'a sound of sheer silence' (1 Kings 19:12) and Paul says that 'in [God] we live and move and have our being' (Acts 17:28).

Enoch 'walked with God' – an echo, perhaps, of God 'walking in the garden'. And because his life is different, his death is also different, holding no fear or pain.

What does it mean to you to 'walk with God'?

VERONICA ZUNDEL

The sorrow of sin

The Lord saw that the wickedness of humankind was great in the earth, and that every inclination of the thoughts of their hearts was only evil continually. And the Lord was sorry that he had made humankind on the earth, and it grieved him to his heart. So the Lord said, 'I will blot out from the earth the human beings I have created – people together with animals and creeping things and birds of the air, for I am sorry that I have made them.' But Noah found favour in the sight of the Lord.

If this were a submission for a creative writing course, the tutor would immediately mark down the first sentence. Too many hyperboles: 'great', 'every', 'only', 'continually'! Yet this style conveys to the reader just how total the corruption of humankind is. It affects thoughts, motivations, actions, relationship with creation. No wonder God appears to be giving up on people…

'It grieved his heart.' The degradation of humanity does not call forth anger in God, but sorrow. It is a picture of a parent whose children have all gone astray, full of pain and regret for the innocence they used to have. And then… there is a 'but'. 'But' is always an interesting word in the Bible, and here the 'but' is that there's a snag in God's plan – there is at least one human who does not deserve to be destroyed. This reminds me of the bargaining between Abraham and God about the fate of Sodom, where God promises not to destroy the city if even ten righteous people are found there – but there are none (Genesis 18:22–32).

If we read the news, or use social media, we might be forgiven for thinking that not much has changed since the days of Noah. Every day there is some new atrocity, tragedy or dodgy dealing to report. We need to be aware, however, that good news rarely sells, and that there are many deeds of compassion and justice going on which we may not hear about. Our world still contains many Noahs.

'The line separating good and evil passes not through states, nor between classes, nor between political parties either – but right through every human heart' (Aleksandr Solzhenitsyn). Do you agree?

VERONICA ZUNDEL

Covenant love

God said to Noah, 'I have determined to make an end of all flesh, for the earth is filled with violence because of them; now I am going to destroy them along with the earth. Make yourself an ark of cypress wood; make rooms in the ark, and cover it inside and out with pitch... For my part, I am going to bring a flood of waters on the earth, to destroy from under heaven all flesh in which is the breath of life; everything that is on the earth shall die. But I will establish my covenant with you; and you shall come into the ark, you, your sons, your wife, and your sons' wives with you. And of every living thing, of all flesh, you shall bring two of every kind into the ark, to keep them alive with you; they shall be male and female.'

We are not told how Noah feels about the destruction of 'all flesh'. Is he sad that his neighbours and perhaps friends will perish? Perhaps it is better not to ask – this is after all a story about the righteousness of God and the unrighteousness of humanity, and its lines are drawn boldly and broadly.

What we do know is that, along with Noah and his family, God plans to rescue breeding pairs of every kind of animal. This, the first plan of salvation in the Bible, is not about rescuing a few humans and letting the rest of creation hang. There is no mandate here for believing that salvation is about snatching a minority of people from the earth and destroying everything else. Instead, there is a clear message that the fate of humans and that of creation are of equal interest to God. Concern for nature is therefore central to our Christian faith.

This is also the first mention in the Bible of a covenant, a solemn agreement, between God and humankind. A covenant is a bond between partners, where each side commits to certain actions and behaviours. You might call it a contract, but it is deeper than that – it is an ongoing relationship, with an emotional and spiritual dimension.

Is there anyone with whom you feel you have a 'covenant'?
Pray for that person.

VERONICA ZUNDEL

Costing not less than everything

The flood continued for forty days on the earth; and the waters increased, and bore up the ark, and it rose high above the earth... But God remembered Noah and all the wild animals and all the domestic animals that were with him in the ark. And God made a wind blow over the earth, and the waters subsided... At the end of forty days Noah opened the window of the ark... and sent out the raven; and it went to and fro until the waters were dried up from the earth. Then he sent out the dove... but the dove found no place to set its foot... He waited another seven days, and again he sent out the dove from the ark; and the dove came back to him in the evening, and there in its beak was a freshly plucked olive leaf; so Noah knew that the waters had subsided from the earth.

My neighbour had a flood last year caused by a blocked bathroom basin. Already traumatised by a horrific bereavement, she was deeply affected by this damage to her home and her sense of security. Even without literal flooding, some people's lives seem to be a constant flood of painful events. And not everyone has an 'ark' – a church community, a supportive family, a circle of friends – to keep their head above the waters.

Noah is safe, but at the cost of everything he has known before: home, neighbours, property, security. To find salvation, he has to leave all else behind. But then, isn't this true for us all? Jesus told his followers: 'For those who want to save their life will lose it, and those who lose their life for my sake will find it' (Matthew 16:25, repeated in all four Gospels). As the disciples commented, 'This is a hard saying.'

Yet really, how secure are we ever, knowing that disaster can strike anyone at any time? Far better to surrender false security for true – for when we are in God's hands, tragedy may still happen, but Emmanuel, God-with-us, is by our side.

If there is part of your life you haven't given to God, pray about it now.
If you feel 'flooded', pray for dry land.

VERONICA ZUNDEL

A sign of commitment

Then God said to Noah and to his sons with him, 'As for me, I am establishing my covenant with you and your descendants after you, and with every living creature that is with you, the birds, the domestic animals, and every animal of the earth with you, as many as came out of the ark. I establish my covenant with you, that never again shall all flesh be cut off by the waters of a flood, and never again shall there be a flood to destroy the earth.' God said, 'This is the sign of the covenant that I make between me and you and every living creature that is with you, for all future generations: I have set my bow in the clouds, and it shall be a sign of the covenant between me and the earth.'

There's a Charles Schulz 'Peanuts' cartoon in which it is raining heavily, and Charlie Brown wonders whether the whole world will be flooded. Linus reminds him of God's promise to Noah. Charlie says, 'You've taken a great weight off my mind.' 'Sound theology has a way of doing that,' answers Linus.

I can remember earnest Christians saying we shouldn't wear rainbow jewellery or clothing because 'It's a New Age symbol'. To offer some 'sound theology', I'd remind them that God got there first! But you can't have the rainbow unless you have both rain and sun. No rain, no rainbow. Or as Julian of Norwich put it, 'Sin is behovely [necessary/inevitable] but all shall be well and all manner of things shall be well.'

I'm currently reading Hannah Hurnard's wonderful allegory *Hind's Feet on High Places* to my neighbour. For (rather unwanted) companions on her journey to the High Places, the Chief Shepherd gives Much-Afraid the veiled figures of Sorrow and Suffering. Yet when she finally reaches the summit, she finds they have transformed into Joy and Peace.

God's covenant is not just with Noah and his family, but 'with every living creature', reinforcing God's love and care for the earth (and why would any artist not love their own works?). Does this apply to the 'new covenant' in Jesus too?

---

*Pray for anyone you know who is going through suffering
(this may include yourself).*

VERONICA ZUNDEL

Drunk and disorderly

Noah, a man of the soil, was the first to plant a vineyard. He drank some of the wine and became drunk, and he lay uncovered in his tent. And Ham, the father of Canaan, saw the nakedness of his father, and told his two brothers outside. Then Shem and Japheth took a garment, laid it on both their shoulders, and walked backwards and covered the nakedness of their father; their faces were turned away, and they did not see their father's nakedness. When Noah awoke from his wine and knew what his youngest son had done to him, he said, 'Cursed be Canaan; lowest of slaves shall he be to his brothers.'

In biblical culture, nakedness brought shame on the person who looked at it, not on the person who was naked. This gives force to Jesus' command, 'From anyone who takes away your coat do not withhold even your shirt' (Luke 6:29); this would leave the person naked and shame the one who had taken the clothes.

So in this strange story, Ham is shamed by his action of seeing his drunken father in the nude – and yet he even boasts of it to his brothers. With Ham's alternative name of 'Canaan', this might have been told to justify the Israelites' capture of Canaanite land as related in later books. It may also have been a warning against drinking too much, which affects the family of the drunkard as much as the one who drinks!

Sadly, it has also been used to justify racism, with 'Ham' standing for darker-skinned races, whom white people regarded as destined by God to be their slaves. This illustrates how dangerous it can be to take isolated bits of the Bible as 'proof texts' to reinforce a view you already hold, rather than seeing the broad themes of the Bible pointing to love of God and neighbour.

What then should we make of Noah's drunkenness? We can certainly see it as a reminder that none of the 'heroes' of the Bible, male or female, are flawless; that even our best deeds are 'like a filthy cloth' (Isaiah 64:6) when compared with God's holiness.

Pray for those addicted to alcohol and for their families and friends.

VERONICA ZUNDEL

Origins

These are the descendants of Noah's sons, Shem, Ham, and Japheth; children were born to them after the flood… The descendants of Ham: Cush, Egypt, Put, and Canaan… Cush became the father of Nimrod; he was the first on earth to become a mighty warrior. He was a mighty hunter before the Lord; therefore it is said, 'Like Nimrod a mighty hunter before the Lord.' The beginning of his kingdom was Babel, Erech, and Accad, all of them in the land of Shinar. From that land he went into Assyria, and built Nineveh, Rehoboth-ir, Calah, and Resen between Nineveh and Calah; that is the great city. Egypt became the father of Ludim, Anamim, Lehabim, Naphtuhim, Pathrusim, Casluhim, and Caphtorim, from which the Philistines come.

'Basil didn't know what "begatting" was, but it seemed there was a lot of it about in those days.' So thinks a small boy in a video by Taffy Davies, on reading passages like this, which in older translations would read 'Cush begat Nimrod… Egypt begat Ludim' and so on. There was indeed 'a lot of it about'!

Biblical genealogies can be baffling or boring to us, though to their original hearers, they were a fascinating account of their ancestors, like the programme *Who Do You Think You Are?* Even now we can pick out highlights. Take Nimrod, a descendant of the 'cursed' Ham: both a hunter and a warrior, he lives by killing; yet he lives 'before the Lord'. For ancient people, hunting and war were about survival, and no one questioned them; for us, who follow the Prince of Peace, it is a different matter.

Then there's the mention of Babel, which will be significant later; and Nineveh, 'the great city' which will feature centrally in the book of Jonah. And Caphtorim (possibly Crete), 'from which the Philistines come'. Major actors in the Old Testament are introduced here.

I suspect the main message we can draw from this is the clear idea that the whole human race, or at least that part of it known to the ancient Jewish people, has a common origin. No one is born superior or inferior.

What ethnic or cultural groups do you find it hard to relate to?
How could you get to know them?

VERONICA ZUNDEL

Bigger than yours

Now the whole earth had one language and the same words. And as they migrated from the east, they came upon a plain in the land of Shinar and settled there… Then they said, 'Come, let us build ourselves a city, and a tower with its top in the heavens, and let us make a name for ourselves; otherwise we shall be scattered abroad upon the face of the whole earth.' … And the Lord said, 'Look, they are one people, and they have all one language; and this is only the beginning of what they will do; nothing that they propose to do will now be impossible for them. Come, let us go down, and confuse their language there, so that they will not understand one another's speech.' So the Lord scattered them abroad from there over the face of all the earth, and they left off building the city.

As the daughter of refugees, I was brought up with two languages. This gave me a lifelong love of words and a head start in learning other languages. The diversity of languages can be seen as a wonderful expression of human creativity. Or we can see it, as here, as a barrier to different peoples understanding each other.

This is another 'origin story', explaining the multitude of languages. As with the sin of Eden, it is a human attempt to 'be like God' – something which, ironically, Genesis 1:27 tells us we already are. Throughout history, humans have always built towers to display wealth and power: think of the Italian town of San Gimignano, a medieval 'tower race', or the competition to build the tallest building in the world.

Why is God here so keen to limit human capabilities, to make it harder for us to work together? No doubt because we have shown ourselves able to unite for great evil (such as the Nazi regime my parents fled). The story of Pentecost, however, where all can understand each other's languages, shows that in the kingdom of God, barriers are broken down and we can work together for great good.

---

*'If I speak in the tongues of mortals and of angels, but do not have love,
I am a noisy gong or a clanging cymbal' (1 Corinthians 13:1).*

VERONICA ZUNDEL

Bread in John

At the Friday market near where I live, there is a wonderful bread stall. Every variety is there, piled high. It always looks and smells delicious. In a poetic moment I once called it 'my idea of heaven'.

Think for a moment of what goes into that loaf on your kitchen table. Sun, rain, soil and seed. Sowing, harvesting, processing and baking. Transporting, shopping and buying. All of life goes into it.

Bread is sometimes called the stuff of life. It is certainly one of the most ancient staple foods. We know Egyptians were baking it around 20BC. We call a wage earner a 'bread winner'. Bread has sometimes been an alternative name for money. 'Bread and water' expresses the most basic, unadorned sustenance we need for life. So when Jesus teaches us to pray for our 'daily bread', it is about our most necessary day-to-day provision, no more, no less. And when he uses bread as an illustration of the life of his kingdom he is telling us there is nothing more basic that we need – Jesus is the bread of life.

But Jesus also speaks of himself as bread and encourages his followers to eat him – using poetic and sacramental language that shocked and puzzled his hearers. 'I am the bread of life.' When he broke bread at the last supper he said, 'This is my body.' Jesus tells us he is the true bread that will feed, sustain and utterly satisfy us. 'Feed me now and ever more,' we sing to him.

But in the stories of Jesus there was the recurring scandal of who he broke bread with, who he sat at table with. Someone once said, 'Jesus was killed because of who he ate with.' The bread is for the hungry. It is food for sinners, outcasts, the unloved and the outsiders.

This fortnight of reflections on bread and Jesus is happening in the midst of a world where many are hungry and go without. To follow Jesus means to share life as he shares it, breaking our bread with others generously, restlessly and discontentedly until all find welcome at the table in his kingdom and are filled at last.

DAVID RUNCORN

Bread in the wilderness

After this Jesus went to the other side of the Sea of Galilee, also called the Sea of Tiberias. A large crowd kept following him, because they saw the signs that he was doing for the sick. Jesus went up the mountain and sat down there with his disciples. Now the Passover, the festival of the Jews, was near.

These verses introduce an extended passage of ministry and teaching about Jesus. Through word and sign – and not without some confusion and fierce disagreement – Jesus is revealing who he really is. And again and again bread will be at the centre of the drama.

John begins by setting the scene very carefully. Jesus has crossed the Sea of Galilee to the far side. He is followed by a large crowd. He goes up a mountain and begins to teach (and we know he will shortly be miraculously feeding 5,000 people in that wilderness place). John also gives us some significant background information. It is near the feast of the Passover at which bread is broken and shared and the story of the deliverance out of slavery in Egypt is relived.

We are meant to be making some connections here. Who else do we know who crossed a sea, led the crowd on the other side, gave them miraculous food in the wilderness and went up a mountain and taught? Of course, it was Moses. The connection between Moses and Jesus is one that all the Gospels make in different ways. John is saying here that Moses and the story of the Exodus and Passover was actually a sign and foreshowing of a greater story of salvation. The time has now come when everything the Exodus story pointed to is coming to fulfilment. Jesus is the 'true' Moses. And Jesus, in his sacrifice on the cross, becomes the true Passover. He is the bread of life.

So it is not only the Passover that is near in this story. In a much deeper and more significant way Jesus is near too. He always is.

As this series begins, what is your prayer to Jesus?

DAVID RUNCORN

What are we going to do?

When he looked up and saw a large crowd coming towards him, Jesus said to Philip, 'Where are we to buy bread for these people to eat?' He said this to test him, for he himself knew what he was going to do. Philip answered him, 'Six months' wages would not buy enough bread for each of them to get a little.'

'What are we going to do?' The question must have startled the disciples. 'You are asking *us*?' But John is clear that Jesus is not asking the question because he needs help. He already knows. He is testing them. And not for the first time the disciples discover that following Jesus leads into situations that are beyond their faith, understanding and imagination. But the test was not to trip them up and leave them embarrassed. They were not expected to solve the problem themselves. The challenge they faced was to trust in God, like Jesus. The effect of their own helplessness is to make an utterly vivid contrast with Jesus' own faith and power to transform the situation.

Philip failed the test emphatically. He could only think in the most practical terms of the money and material resources. That will sound all too familiar to many churches today wondering how to respond to the huge challenges of our times and where to find enough to offer 'the crowds' of our day. But the only real failure is not to learn. As Philip looked back on this conversation from the other side of the miracle that was about to happen, surrounded by crowds full of food and running out of baskets to gather all the leftovers in, we might wonder what he had learnt.

Perhaps he learned that the challenge is not to look at the size of the crowd? That the size of a bank balance is not relevant either? That it is not about us at all?

The challenge is to have faith in God. And to trust that now, as then, Jesus knows what he is going to do.

Lord, help us to trust and have faith as you did.

DAVID RUNCORN

When it all feels inadequate

One of his disciples, Andrew, Simon Peter's brother, said to him, 'There is a boy here who has five barley loaves and two fish. But what are they among so many people?' Jesus said, 'Make the people sit down.' Now there was a great deal of grass in the place; so they sat down, about five thousand in all. Then Jesus took the loaves, and when he had given thanks, he distributed them to those who were seated, so also the fish, as much as they wanted.

After Philip's financial despair, Andrew comes to Jesus. He has found a boy in the crowd with some food. All the Gospels tell the miracle of the feeding of the crowd. Only John's account mentions this 'lad'. Perhaps it was his packed lunch; some suggest he was a vendor. If this is so then he has nearly sold out. Barley loaves were the very cheapest kind of bread. The fish described would have been small – dried or pickled. It is a meagre offering. This is the food of the poor and barely sufficient, even then. So, even when some food supplies are found, they are of impoverished quality and, as Andrew acknowledges, completely inadequate for what is needed.

What the little boy makes of all this we are not told. He may only be aware that someone is after his food. Imagine him standing before Jesus with his few loaves and fishes with a huge, hungry crowd surrounding them. But Jesus does not laugh or mock at what has been brought to him. Considering what an amazing miracle this is, John's telling of it is matter-of-fact. Jesus just takes the food, says grace and gives it out to 5,000 people! And from that tiny offering, received and blessed with divine gratitude, all are fed and satisfied.

There are few churches today that cannot relate to Andrew's awareness that what he has to offer is painfully inadequate for the needs of the moment. It is very easy to be discouraged and lose heart. But Jesus receives our hesitant, limited offerings as he received the little boy's. He says thank you for it. And would you believe? – it is more than enough.

Today, Lord, I offer you the little I feel I have.

DAVID RUNCORN

Divine improvisation

One of his disciples, Andrew, Simon Peter's brother, said to him, 'There is a boy here who has five barley loaves and two fish. But what are they among so many people?' Jesus said, 'Make the people sit down.' Now there was a great deal of grass in the place; so they sat down, about five thousand in all. Then Jesus took the loaves, and when he had given thanks, he distributed them to those who were seated, so also the fish, as much as they wanted.

When did you last have to prepare a meal in a hurry for unexpected visitors? Was there mild panic and quick thinking? An anxious look in the fridge or cupboard? Adapting, improvising and hoping there will be enough to go round? Well, this even happens to Jesus, it seems. The other Gospel accounts make clear that the reason Jesus and the disciples had gone to the other side of the lake was to get some quiet and rest. They were exhausted. But it didn't work. The crowd found them. And one result of this was the urgent need for food for a very large number of people.

A study of Christian discipleship and ministry describes it as being a work of 'faithful improvisation'. I like that. Life rarely happens in ideal circumstances. It requires the willingness and ability to work faithfully with whatever is to hand.

I love the thought that Jesus is an improviser too. He too is willing and able to work with whatever is to hand. He does it here. In the face of the unexpected crowd (and one they had been trying to avoid) he lovingly improvises. Working with pitifully inadequate resources, Jesus provides more than enough for all.

This is a more exciting way of thinking of God's presence and work in the world and in our lives than if he simply knows everything in advance. For someone who can improvise, all things are possible. Imagination and flexibility is all. 'Let there be...' said God in the creation story. But was that really the work of a prearranged fixed agenda? Or was this the generous, divine imagination out of which all things are possible from whatever is offered?

Today, Lord, may I improvise with your imaginative love.

DAVID RUNCORN

More than enough

When they were satisfied, he told his disciples, 'Gather up the fragments left over, so that nothing may be lost.'... They filled twelve baskets. When the people saw the sign that he had done, they began to say, 'This is indeed the prophet who is to come into the world.' When Jesus realized that they were about to come and take him by force to make him king, he withdrew by himself.

The meal is over and everyone is full up. With a crowd that size, it might have taken a while to realise something extraordinary had been happening. The food just kept coming, But where from, out here in the middle of nowhere? The word goes round that it is Jesus who has done this.

'Gather up the fragments left over,' says Jesus. The word used here was used in the Exodus story when the people gathered up the manna in the wilderness. What is this about? Twelve baskets probably symbolise the twelve tribes – the whole people of God. His concern is not litter. Nothing must perish. In other places in his ministry, Jesus expresses his longing that no one is lost or perishes. In John the focus of his ministry is also described as a gathering together – uniting all in the love he and the Father share.

That so much is left over after everyone had more than enough emphasises the wonderful generosity of Jesus. The extravagance of God is where John's Gospel starts. The first sign Jesus did at a wedding was to turn a huge quantity of water into wine after they had all drunk their fill (John 2). God's feeding and sustaining is for all. None must be left to perish. There is more than enough. All must be gathered in.

But here, as elsewhere, the miracle becomes a distraction and his ministry is misunderstood. No one is listening. He cannot be on demand. They must lose their image of a messiah who just fills their hunger and meets their need – and so must we. If there are times he must withdraw it is for our sake.

Lord, thank you for being so generous to us.

DAVID RUNCORN

Into the storm

When evening came, his disciples went down to the lake, got into a boat, and started across the lake to Capernaum. It was now dark, and Jesus had not yet come to them. The lake became rough because a strong wind was blowing. When they had rowed about three or four miles, they saw Jesus walking on the lake and coming near the boat, and they were terrified. But he said to them, 'It is I; do not be afraid.' Then they wanted to take him into the boat, and immediately the boat reached the land towards which they were going.

In the middle of a passage about Jesus and bread is a story about the disciples getting caught in a storm at night. The sea that the disciples had so recently crossed with Jesus, and without incident, has now turned dark, stormy and frightening without him. They are even terrified when Jesus appears. Nothing is secure. And they are unable to reach the shore.

Finding this story in the midst of important teaching about Jesus and who he is, is surely significant. The disciples' struggle to cross the sea offers a dramatic parable for the journey of following and understanding they are embarked on. It is our journey too. We can speak too carelessly about conversion and following Jesus as if it is an experience of light, joy and understanding. That is certainly part of it. But by contrast the writer C.S. Lewis wrote of 'the harrowing operation of conversion'. This story reminds us how often following Jesus left the disciples frightened, confused, bewildered and in the dark.

The Christian journey of faith and discipleship involves such a total change of heart and mind that we should not be surprised if we feel like the disciples in that boat at times. The journey can be turbulent and dark and we feel lost and powerless. For such times the message of this story is both uncompromisingly honest and very reassuring. It is only with Jesus the disciples reach the journey's end safely. They had begun the journey without him actually. And where is Jesus? He is there – in the midst of the storm, walking towards them.

Lord, when it is stormy and dark, help me to trust you.

DAVID RUNCORN

Coming back for more

'Very truly, I tell you, you are looking for me, not because you saw signs, but because you ate your fill of the loaves. Do not work for the food that perishes, but for the food that endures for eternal life, which the Son of Man will give you.'

The crowd have come back for more. Are we surprised? They had been wonderfully fed the last time. The miracle was amazing. Exciting things happen when this person Jesus is around. But they were only after more of the same. They could not see beyond the sign to the greater reality it pointed to. 'You just want to be filled again,' says Jesus. It is thoughtless behaviour.

Does this sound familiar? Our Western lifestyle has been described as 'living on the compass of our excitement'. We go looking wherever the needle points to new excitement or satisfaction. And it changes regularly. We get bored quickly and are easily distracted. It means our appetites live on a constant level of overstimulation. We are compulsive consumers and we find it hard to sustain concentration for any length of time. Even approaches to church can be shaped around what we want, enjoy and find exciting.

An important mark of coming to maturity involves learning to practise what psychologists call 'delayed gratification'. An earliest memory of this challenge for me was the awful struggle on school outings not to eat my packed lunch before the coach had even left the school car park. Life demands the willingness and ability to deny ourselves more immediate, short-term satisfactions without which we will never become part of the bigger, more glorious story God has for us.

One of the temptations Jesus wrestled with in his humanity was not to be driven by a search for immediate satisfaction and immediate needs. Being hungry and needing food to eat is not wrong. But there are times it must wait. He knew his deepest hunger and priority must be for the food only God can give. He must put God first. And we must learn the same.

Lord, teach me to wait beyond my short-term excitements and appetites.

DAVID RUNCORN

Learning to wait

'Very truly, I tell you, you are looking for me, not because you saw signs, but because you ate your fill of the loaves. Do not work for the food that perishes, but for the food that endures for eternal life, which the Son of Man will give you.'

Do not work for what cannot last, says Jesus. Elsewhere, Jesus teaches us to be very practical in praying for our 'daily bread'. That too is within God's loving concern. But if that is all we focus on, we will miss what gives our lives their richest and most glorious meaning. There is a food that endures, says Jesus.

The ancient discipline of fasting has always been a practical way of doing this. The motive is important. We do not deny ourselves food because this appetite is wrong or sinful. When we fast we are saying that our earthly appetites and desires have their place. There is a time and place for them. But they must not be allowed to control or distract us. By not immediately satisfying them with what perishes, our longings can deepen for what is most truly enduring. Fasting can take different forms. It could be time away from TV or social media as well as food. It is often only when we fast that we discover how deeply our life habits have become our drivers.

There was a time when Christians were taught to fast before receiving communion at church on Sundays. It might be a discipline to relearn. It expresses what we put first in our lives. Other hungers must wait. There is food, there is sustenance, that earthly food and satisfactions are no substitute for. We must fast for the bread that comes down from heaven and endures.

I remember an older Christian telling me how much it meant to him that the first food that passed his lips each Sunday was the bread of life – the body of Christ. In that moment he was expressing the heart of his faith – the priority of living from what God alone can give.

Lord, help me to put you first.

DAVID RUNCORN

Food for the journey

Jesus said to them, 'Very truly, I tell you, it was not Moses who gave you the bread from heaven, but it is my Father who gives you the true bread from heaven. For the bread of God is that which comes down from heaven and gives life to the world.' They said to him, 'Sir, give us this bread always.' Jesus said to them, 'I am the bread of life. Whoever comes to me will never be hungry, and whoever believes in me will never be thirsty.'

In J.R.R. Tolkien's epic fantasy trilogy *The Lord of the Rings*, the Elves of Lothlórien give the Fellowship of the Ring a special food for their long and dangerous journey. It is called Lembas – a light 'waybread' to sustain travellers on the way. It is no ordinary bread. It is marvellously nutritious; just one of the thin cakes is enough for a whole day's march. And it does not just satisfy physical hunger; a piece of this and strength and hope are renewed in even the most desperate places. Lembas is offensive to evil creatures. Offered compassionately to Gollum, he chokes on a crumb of it and would rather starve than eat it. Without faith, it is bitter and inedible.

In the older Catholic tradition, communion was called *viaticum*, meaning 'for the way'. Communion bread is the spiritual food for the Christian's arduous journey through earthly life to heaven.

Today, around the world, bread for the way is being broken and shared in many different places – at high altars, in a prison cell, in refugee camps, beside hospital beds. In each of these places, Christ, the true bread, will be present, renewing life, will and hope.

Lord, feed me for the way today, and give me faith to accept the bread that you offer.

DAVID RUNCORN

Heaven and earth

Then the Jews began to complain about him because he said, 'I am the bread that came down from heaven.' They were saying, 'Is not this Jesus, the son of Joseph, whose father and mother we know? How can he now say, "I have come down from heaven"?'

We do not know what it was like to be living in Jesus' village when he was growing up. Some 'unofficial' accounts of his childhood tell stories of him effortlessly creating birds and animals out of the dust of the earth and such like. But his critics here speak as if he has not stood out in any way, though we know from other stories that by the age of twelve he was showing exceptional wisdom.

At what point did Jesus know he was 'from above' – to use the imagery in John's Gospel? Was he aware from day one of his life, 'I am God. I am the Messiah'? Or did he grow up always knowing the love of his heavenly Father and the life of the Spirit alongside that of his earthly family? Perhaps he became slowly and painfully aware that what was so utterly natural and obvious to him was not apparent at all to those around him.

The story is told of a world in which everyone has eyes but cannot see. This happened so long ago there is no memory or awareness of what sight is. Their sightless world is 'normal'. Into this world comes someone who can see. He lives, speaks and acts out of a whole dimension of awareness that others simply don't have and cannot understand. They cannot accept him and he is violently expelled from the land.

Later in Jesus' ministry, people's eyes were opened to new life when he broke bread with them. In this passage bread from heaven is a poetic way of expressing the life he came down to offer through sharing of his own flesh and blood. His life is the food which opens eyes, awakens hearts and breaks open the sightless life of earth to the vision of heaven.

Lord, thank you for enduring misunderstanding and scorn for us.

DAVID RUNCORN

This is my body

'Those who eat my flesh and drink my blood abide in me, and I in them. Just as the living Father sent me, and I live because of the Father, so whoever eats me will live because of me. This is the bread that came down from heaven, not like that which your ancestors ate, and they died. But the one who eats this bread will live for ever.'

Earlier in this chapter Jesus provided the food to eat. Now the language changes quite dramatically; Jesus is now the food itself. Those listening to him found the idea of eating his flesh and blood utterly shocking. By the end of this teaching, even some of his disciples will have given up following him. How does this language leave you feeling?

The early Christians were accused of cannibalism because they spoke of eating the flesh of Jesus. But it is Jesus himself who teaches this. It means the heart of our faith is this: a participation in the suffering, death and resurrection of Christ. This language links the communion meal totally and unmistakably with the cross. Those who eat his flesh and blood identify with one who suffered, died and was raised. One of the traditional names for the communion service is the Lord's supper. With this language, Jesus is saying 'Yes, it is my supper. And I am the meal. It is my flesh and blood you eat and drink. This is my body.'

There is another reflection to offer on this uncomfortable passage. We expect the food we eat to become part of us. But Jesus feeds us with his own flesh and blood so that we might become part of him, united with him. Jesus calls this 'abiding'. It is a tender image that expresses a sense of being deeply at home in a place or relationship. Jesus would unite us in his own body. If the language of flesh and blood reveals the cost of this gift of himself to us, the word 'abiding' expresses the gift itself.

Lord, as you offer yourself to me, make me like you.

DAVID RUNCORN

Betrayal

'I am not speaking of all of you; I know whom I have chosen. But it is to fulfil the scripture, "The one who ate my bread has lifted his heel against me."'

The quotation here is from Psalm 49. We do not know the story, but the psalmist is grieving over a betrayal by a close companion. The image of the lifted heel comes from rural life. Imagine you have a horse that you have raised, cared for, groomed and loved. Then one day, inexplicably, as you turn to leave after feeding it, it lifts its back leg and kicks out at you viciously.

If nothing else, this quotation expresses how closely Jesus feels he has shared his life with Judas, who is now about to betray him. The word 'companion' actually comes from two Latin words *com* and *panis* – literally 'with bread'. A friend is one you break bread with.

Perhaps you have experienced a relationship painfully breaking down like this? For Christians this can be all the more devastating. Aren't we called to love each other? For several periods of my life I have lived in Christian communities. I recall how shared living starts with high idealism – 'If we can't live the gospel here, where can it be lived?' But we soon discover how easily love runs out, how complex our motives are, how misguided our best intentions – and we must learn the way of forgiveness. A faith with a cross at its centre surely warns us this must be so. We must never underestimate the depths from which we need redeeming.

When a friendship broke down, I felt my faith had completely failed and that I should not even be receiving communion. But it was there God spoke to me. It was in the moment in the service when the bread is broken and we say, 'We break this bread to share in the body of Christ.' We meet and receive Christ in the brokenness of things – in all the fragility of human love and belonging. We meet in the breaking of the bread. There is nowhere else.

Lord, meet me in broken things today.

DAVID RUNCORN

Honouring

Jesus was troubled in spirit, and declared, 'Very truly, I tell you, one of you will betray me.' [One of his disciples asked him,] 'Lord, who is it?' Jesus answered, 'It is the one to whom I give this piece of bread when I have dipped it in the dish.' So when he had dipped the piece of bread, he gave it to Judas son of Simon Iscariot.

At a certain point in the meal, Jesus becomes visibly distressed. This word was used of him by Lazarus's grave and then when he was contemplating his own death in Gethsemane. Here the distress is brought on by the knowledge that he is about to be betrayed by one of his own disciples.

And what happens next? In Passover meals there is a moment when the host takes a piece of bread, dips it into the sauce of one of the dishes and offers it to a guest who may be present or perhaps to their spouse. It is a gesture of honouring and respect. Jesus now dips the bread and offers it to – Judas. At one level it changes nothing. Judas goes straight out to arrange his betrayal. But it means that in the last moment Judas shares with Jesus before he does so, Jesus reaches out to him in companionship, with a gesture that expresses love, acceptance and honour. His betrayer is still his beloved.

We do not know what led Judas to do what he did. But how amazing that even his betrayal, like human sin, comes to serve the purposes of God. That is why in the ancient Easter liturgy the church cries out, 'O happy fault that won for us so great a salvation!'

A few verses later, as Jesus hangs on the cross he is heard to pray, 'Father forgive, they do not know what they are doing.' That prayer of love surely included Judas as he descended into his own terrible turmoil and despair.

Lord, thank you for where your word of forgiveness will be heard today.

DAVID RUNCORN

Restoration of Peter

Just after daybreak, Jesus stood on the beach; but the disciples did not know that it was Jesus… That disciple whom Jesus loved said to Peter, 'It is the Lord!' When Simon Peter heard that it was the Lord, he put on some clothes, for he was naked, and jumped into the lake… When they had gone ashore, they saw a charcoal fire there, with fish on it, and bread… Jesus came and took the bread and gave it to them.

This is a particularly poignant scene. It is the other side of Easter, but the disciples have been unable to grasp what has happened. Bewildered and confused, some of them, led by Peter, have gone back to fishing, but have caught nothing. Even their old way of life is empty. They are caught between life and death and at home in neither.

But the story now focuses on Peter. A stranger on the shore tells them to fish on 'the other side' and now their nets nearly burst. When Peter learns it is Jesus, he is desperately eager to reach him. He dresses and jumps into the water, leaving the rest to follow. What was he feeling? This is a man who had betrayed and deserted Jesus just days before.

There on the shore, two things are specifically mentioned. A charcoal fire; the word for this fire is the same one used of the fire Peter was standing by at the High Priest's house as he denied knowing Jesus three times. Peter must come to that fire again. He must return to the place of his betrayal. He must face what he has done. There is no running away if we wish to receive God's love. We must bring it all – even our betrayal and faithlessness.

And there is the bread. It would awaken memories of the last supper – this is my body; and of other meals and miracles and teachings.

As this fortnight comes to a close, why not take a piece of bread and ask yourself in what new ways it now speaks of you of Jesus, the bread of life.

DAVID RUNCORN

Crowds

Wherever Jesus went, he was surrounded by people. Only occasionally could he escape from them, retreating into the wilderness to find time to pray, seeking out quiet places where he could be alone and still, to listen to God's voice and be resourced for the demands that were made upon him. The rest of the time the crowds pressed upon him, surrounding him with their questions and demands, their adoration and hostility. The crowd is referred to as *ochlos* in New Testament Greek – it is a different word to that used in the Old Testament for the Children of Israel, because the people who made up the crowd are a mixed bunch of Jews and Gentiles, rich and poor, peasants and city dwellers. They all had one thing in common, however: the opportunity to listen to Jesus and to choose the way in which they would respond to his words.

The relationship Jesus had with the group of people who gathered around him, some following him from place to place, others simply meeting him as he arrived at their home village or town, is a rich one. On the part of Jesus, it is a relationship filled with love and compassion, deeply understanding and sensitive to the needs of every individual within the crowd. On the part of the crowd, the response is varied and confused, often intense but rarely unmoved.

As we discover the different attitudes and responses within the crowd to Jesus' words and teaching, we can take time to ask ourselves where we might be in that crowd. How do we react to Jesus? Are our reactions always the same, or do they change? How are we affected by those around us – are our opinions influenced by others or are we able to listen to what Jesus is saying to us without being swayed by group emotions or sentiment? And always we can wonder at the nature and scope of a love which can embrace a hostile crowd chanting for death, seek out an individual hidden in a mass of people who reaches out in fear and faith, and share with all who care to listen, the nature of God's kingdom.

SALLY WELCH

'Sheep without a shepherd'

Then Jesus went about all the cities and villages, teaching in their synagogues, and proclaiming the good news of the kingdom, and curing every disease and every sickness. When he saw the crowds, he had compassion for them, because they were harassed and helpless, like sheep without a shepherd. Then he said to his disciples, 'The harvest is plentiful, but the labourers are few; therefore ask the Lord of the harvest to send out labourers into his harvest.'

One of the most marvellous aspects of Jesus' relationship with the crowds is the deep love he had for all who met him. Time and again we are reminded of the compassion Jesus felt for the people he was teaching, and this situation is no different. Jesus feels pity for the crowd, 'harassed and helpless, like sheep without a shepherd'. What a powerful simile this is! Anyone who has seen a flock of panicked sheep will have been struck by the way these poor beasts run frantically in all directions, their short, stiff legs struggling to keep up with the fear which is propelling their large clumsy bodies across the fields, stopping and changing direction for no apparent reason before gathering perhaps, trembling and huddled together in a corner. Only the trusted voice of their shepherd can induce them out of their positions as he reassures them, calming their fears with his steady voice, leading them to a place of real safety.

So too are we inclined to allow our fears – real or imagined – to rule our lives, letting them drive us into unconsidered actions, or attitudes of unnecessary anxiety. Too often our fears are fed by the actions of others around us – media reports which magnify every disaster, doomsayers amongst our community or friends and, most powerful of all, the inner voice of our insecurity, which predicts only the worst outcomes. Then we need to pause and allow ourselves a moment of stillness and quiet so that we can hear the voice of our shepherd, full of compassion and understanding for our plight, reassuring us of the constancy of his love and the eternity of his presence.

'The Lord is my shepherd: I shall not want' (Psalm 23:1, KJV).

SALLY WELCH

The salt of the earth

'You are the salt of the earth; but if salt has lost its taste, how can its saltiness be restored? It is no longer good for anything, but is thrown out and trampled under foot. You are the light of the world. A city built on a hill cannot be hidden. No one after lighting a lamp puts it under the bushel basket, but on the lampstand, and it gives light to all in the house. In the same way, let your light shine before others, so that they may see your good works and give glory to your Father in heaven.'

Born ten years later than our first three children, our younger son is utterly devoted to his older brother and sisters. It is to them he looks for examples of how to live in this complicated, demanding world we have constructed for our young people, and to do them credit they have always tried to model appropriate ways of dealing with life in the 21st century, aware that what they do is being observed and copied by the one who follows after. Occasionally, however, it is not enough simply to live the life, but talking about motives and attitudes becomes necessary as well. Conversations have been held on a wide range of subjects which provide points of reference for a boy growing into a young man.

Jesus too spent time with people, living his life in a way that acted as an example for them to follow. But sometimes it was necessary to articulate what he meant by the kingdom of God, to make them wonder and reflect, leading them along unfamiliar thought pathways to new insights and understanding. Many of us hesitate to teach what we know about the kingdom of God to others. But we are the 'salt of the earth', the 'light of the world' – a huge responsibility, awesome in its scope. We have a duty not to hide in silence, but to speak out on behalf of our faith, directing the gaze of others so that they too may see the glory of the kingdom.

How might I speak today in ways which promote the kingdom?

SALLY WELCH

The invitation

A man was there named Zacchaeus; he was a chief tax collector and was rich. He was trying to see who Jesus was, but on account of the crowd he could not, because he was short in stature. So he ran ahead and climbed a sycamore tree to see him, because he was going to pass that way. When Jesus came to the place, he looked up and said to him, 'Zacchaeus, hurry and come down; for I must stay at your house today.' So he hurried down and was happy to welcome him.

I recently took a school assembly on the story of Zacchaeus. A small boy played the part of Zacchaeus and the tallest children in the school were the crowd, shutting Zacchaeus out, preventing him from seeing Jesus. I told them how unpopular Zacchaeus would have been, because as well as collecting taxes on behalf of the occupying forces of the Romans, there was a good chance that Zacchaeus would have taken an additional percentage for himself.

We discussed what might have made Zacchaeus behave the way he did and the children suggested all sorts of reasons – perhaps because he was angry at something that had happened to him, perhaps because he was sad. We talked about the way in which sadness and anger can generate vicious circles of unloving and unlovable behaviour. Jesus broke Zacchaeus out of this circle of destructive behaviour by stepping inside it and reaching out to him, offering him acceptance and inclusion. Jesus' attitude towards all people was one of invitation – 'Hurry down' becomes 'come and see', 'follow me'.

We are all invited to become part of an ever-widening circle, a group that includes all who wish to belong, which reaches beyond the group to embrace everyone. An inviting heart dares to break the bonds of anger, bitterness and hurt which hold us captive to destructive ways of living and being. Loving acceptance paves the way for transformation and response.

Heavenly Father, give me a heart that is open to the invitation of your love. May my response be to invite others in turn to acknowledge their position as one of your children and to turn to you with open hearts and minds.

SALLY WELCH

Every person matters

As he went, the crowds pressed in on him. Now there was a woman who had been suffering from haemorrhages for twelve years; and though she had spent all she had on physicians, no one could cure her. She came up behind him and touched the fringe of his clothes, and immediately her haemorrhage stopped. Then Jesus asked, 'Who touched me?' When all denied it, Peter said, 'Master, the crowds surround you and press in on you.' But Jesus said, 'Someone touched me; for I noticed that power had gone out from me.' When the woman saw that she could not remain hidden, she came trembling; and falling down before him, she declared in the presence of all the people why she had touched him, and how she had been immediately healed. He said to her, 'Daughter, your faith has made you well; go in peace.'

On several occasions I have had the privilege of helping out at Christian festivals or events, welcoming guest speakers. In this way I have met many remarkable and talented people, the best of whom being those who acknowledge the people patiently standing in line outside the venue, who listen to their enthusiastic fans, who engage seriously with questions, never showing their boredom or fatigue but offering each person a generous hearing. These speakers make an event an occasion of grace, a demonstration of gospel values, a 'kingdom' time.

Wherever he went, Jesus was besieged by those who wanted something from him. From some came requests for healing, others sought a leader for rebellion and revolution, still others a scapegoat; someone to blame for their fears and disillusionment. Through them all, Jesus moved with graciousness, teaching and loving, recognising the frailty and needs of the individuals who surrounded him. It is when we stop seeing people as individuals and begin instead to see them as groups, as masses, as numbers, that our humanity is threatened. Christianity is a faith which honours the small, the insignificant in the world's eyes – the tiny child, the widow and her mite, the repentant tax collector and the woman in pain. All are worthy in God's eyes, all are loved, all matter.

Heavenly Father, help us to look upon each other with your eyes.

SALLY WELCH

'He said this to test him'

When he looked up and saw a large crowd coming towards him, Jesus said to Philip, 'Where are we to buy bread for these people to eat?' He said this to test him, for he himself knew what he was going to do. Philip answered him, 'Six months' wages would not buy enough bread for each of them to get a little.' One of his disciples, Andrew, Simon Peter's brother, said to him, 'There is a boy here who has five barley loaves and two fish. But what are they among so many people?'

From the beginning of his ministry, Jesus took care to gather round him a small group of people to whom he could give particular attention. It is this group that would be sent out to spread the news of God's love for all people and it was essential that they grasped the message fully and properly before they were charged with its transmission. Too few to be categorised as a crowd, they were in fact often in opposition to the crowd – defending Jesus from its opportuning, protecting his space, enabling his passage. Jesus in his turn used the relationship of his disciples with the crowd to teach them not only about the kingdom of heaven but about themselves as well. Sadly, it seems as if more teaching is needed, for neither Philip nor Andrew can see past the practical challenges of trying to feed so many people, supplied with neither sufficient money or food. For all their willingness to address the problem, they are constrained by their lack of faith – despite the miracles they have witnessed, they still do not expect them.

So too are we in danger of failing to allow ourselves to be guided by faith. So too do we try and confine God within the barriers of our narrow expectations, restricting him to the limits of our own capabilities rather than looking beyond them to the reality of his power.

Almighty God, help me to look above and beyond the smallness of my nature to catch a glimpse of the glory of yours.

SALLY WELCH

'Who do you say that I am?'

Once when Jesus was praying alone, with only the disciples near him, he asked them, 'Who do the crowds say that I am?' They answered, 'John the Baptist; but others, Elijah; and still others that one of the ancient prophets has arisen.' He said to them, 'But who do you say that I am?' Peter answered, 'The Messiah of God.'

As a student, I worked for one summer as a museum attendant at the Ashmolean Museum in Oxford. Set to guarding the galleries for long hours, I would while away the time by imagining the lives of the visitors who came to gaze upon the pictures and statues. However, despite my close attention to those who entered my gallery, I would never recognise the often extremely well-known personalities who would visit. Not until I was having coffee in the staff room and a breathless fellow attendant would ask me, 'Did you see X?', would I realise that I had once again failed to spot a famous film star or television personality.

My failure was not significant – that of the crowds surrounding Jesus was more so. Even when the Messiah himself walks among them, he is not recognised. Mistaken for John the Baptist or one of the prophets, it is only Peter whose eyes are opened to the truth.

One of the tasks of Christians today is to recognise the works and words of God in this world. We are called to identify signs of the kingdom here amongst us and to bring them to the attention of others. We have a duty to look upon the actions of those around us with clear eyes, ready to see the reality of God's love as it is unfolded in the lives that surround us. We must seize upon hope and love and draw the attention of others towards them, not allowing ourselves to be overwhelmed by the darkness, but constantly seeking the light.

Jesus, light of the world, help me to recognise you in the words and actions of those around me and to speak the truth about them.

SALLY WELCH

Withdrawal

But now more than ever the word about Jesus spread abroad; many crowds would gather to hear him and to be cured of their diseases. But he would withdraw to deserted places and pray.

I have always struggled with the concept of 'quiet time'. Happiest when I am surrounded by people, I prefer almost any activity in the company of others rather than being alone. My most creative ideas originate in conversations with others, when plans and projects are formed from many voices and not just one – even when I write, I prefer to do so in a busy café rather than my own quiet study.

But, every now and then, I am reminded of the need to take some time away from the company of others, to withdraw to a quiet place and to listen for the word of God, which can so easily be drowned out by the demands and clatter of everyday life. In doing so, I try deliberately to follow the example set by Christ, the pattern for our lives. Pressed upon by all sides, constantly sought out by those in need and those who simply wanted to spend time in his company, Jesus made it a priority to spend time in deserted places. Only when he was alone could the time and space be found for deep reflection. Only in silence could the voice of God be heard – that still small voice which can so easily be ignored when it is put into competition against the noisy clamour of today's world.

It can be difficult to set time aside and, even when we finally are alone, it can be challenging to stop our mind from flitting here and there, chasing trivial thoughts like so many dancing butterflies rather than paying attention to God. But we must keep trying and offer our attempts, however fractured and feeble, to God, knowing that in his generosity he will bless our efforts and return them in grace a thousand times greater.

Breathe through the heats of our desire
thy coolness and thy balm;
let sense be dumb, let flesh retire;
speak through the earthquake, wind, and fire,
O still, small voice of calm.
(John Whittier, 1872)

SALLY WELCH

Storytelling

He was teaching and saying, 'Is it not written, "My house shall be called a house of prayer for all the nations"? But you have made it a den of robbers.' And when the chief priests and the scribes heard it, they kept looking for a way to kill him; for they were afraid of him, because the whole crowd was spellbound by his teaching.

At a conference recently, one of the optional workshops was entitled simply 'Storytelling'. Curious, I went along and found myself sitting on the floor in a circle of other delegates, listening enraptured as a storyteller told us tales from the Bible. Familiar as these tales were to all those present, the storyteller's words, given emphasis by his voice and actions, held us captive for over an hour, and it was with a sense of leaving an enchanted world that we moved on to the next conference session.

When faced with the decision of how to tell the people he loved about the kingdom of God, Jesus did not hesitate to use stories as his medium. Taking everyday incidents, familiar to his audience, he took his listeners along well-trodden pathways which gradually took new directions. Thus almost imperceptibly the audience would be led to look upon new truths or examine old truths in a new light. Assumptions would be overturned, minds working in rigid patterns shown freedom, new attitudes offered for exploration. Not all of Jesus' stories were easy to understand, but although he left some deliberately obscure, others held a simple directness which led straight to the heart of the matter

Those of us who are familiar with the stories of Jesus almost to the point of boredom can run the risk of neglecting them. It can be very rewarding to take time simply to reread the parables of Jesus in new and perhaps unfamiliar Bible versions – or to be more adventurous still and try cartoon versions, or listening to them read aloud. Better still practise telling the stories in your own words, ready to pass them on to others who are less familiar with the power of the truth contained within them.

'Tell your children of it, and let your children tell their children, and their children another generation' (Joel 1:3, NRSV).

SALLY WELCH

An instrument of praise

He then said to the paralytic – 'Stand up, take your bed and go to your home.' And he stood up and went to his home. When the crowds saw it, they were filled with awe, and they glorified God, who had given such authority to human beings.

When I was training for ordination, I took a placement at an army training barracks, shadowing a Regular Army Chaplain. Andrew was the most cheerful man I had ever met, filled with an infectious joy and a determination to share the gospel with everyone he met. The soldiers in his care, a generally cynical bunch, laughed at his enthusiasm and made fun of his efforts at evangelism, but if they were in trouble or upset, he would be their first port of call. He made no secret of the foundation of his approach – his whole life, he regularly declared, was one of gratitude for his sins forgiven. 'I did terrible things in my youth,' he told me. 'Things which darkened my soul. But I met Jesus and he freed me. I will spend the rest of my life repaying that gift.'

Since Padre Andrew, I have met other men and women whose lives have been transformed by God's grace. Physically healed, mentally freed, all released from burdens which they believed they would carry forever, their love for God is wholehearted and infectious – it is a privilege to know them and a joy to be with them.

The crowd that witnessed Jesus' actions that day so long ago responded to the miracle of sins forgiven, a paralytic healed, in a spontaneous demonstration of worship; being 'filled with awe', they didn't seek scientific or physiological reasons for the miracle which had taken place before their eyes, but instead directed their praise and worship to the one from whom all good things originate.

Amazing grace! How sweet the sound,
That saved a wretch like me!
I once was lost but now am found,
Was blind but now I see.
(John Newton, 1779)

SALLY WELCH

A means of protection

'Have you not read this scripture: "The stone that the builders rejected has become the cornerstone; this was the Lord's doing, and it is amazing in our eyes"?' When they realized that [Jesus] had told this parable against them, they wanted to arrest him, but they feared the crowd. So they left him and went away.

Jesus has arrived in Jerusalem and news of his arrival has spread. He has visited the temple courts and annoyed the chief priests and elders by overturning the tables of the money lenders who were installed there. He has sidestepped the attempts of the authorities to trick him into blasphemy and has instead responded with a parable directed against them. The temple authorities are enraged by this and would love nothing more than to have Jesus arrested, but they are powerless against the crowds whose reaction to this act they fear would be hostile. It is a moment of irony for those of us who read about this incident knowing what will happen to Jesus in the future. The very crowd which in this episode offers protection to Jesus against the chief priests and elders will later hand him over to be killed by the same authorities, adding insult to injury by asking for another criminal to be released rather than him.

The tide of public opinion is well known to be a fickle one. The celebrities who are feted in today's newspapers and magazines are vilified in the very same journals only a few days or weeks later. A decision which might be taken to gain public support can prove to be the very event which secures the dismissal of a government or official figure.

In our personal and work lives alike, we must take account of the effect of public opinion on our actions. We would be foolish to ignore it, but we should also be aware of its fickle nature. The decisions we make should be made in the light of the truth that, ultimately, we are answerable only to God.

It's God we are answerable to – all the way from life to death
and everything in between' (Romans 14:8, THE MESSAGE).

SALLY WELCH

Reluctant to be changed

'Now the parable is this: The seed is the word of God. The ones on the path are those who have heard; then the devil comes and takes away the word from their hearts, so that they may not believe and be saved. The ones on the rock are those who, when they hear the word, receive it with joy. But these have no root; they believe only for a while and in a time of testing fall away. As for what fell among the thorns, these are the ones who hear; but as they go on their way, they are choked by the cares and riches and pleasures of life, and their fruit does not mature. But as for that in the good soil, these are the ones who, when they hear the word, hold it fast in an honest and good heart, and bear fruit with patient endurance.'

What a surprise the words of Jesus must have been to those first listeners. Here was a man who talked of the love of God, not of his judgement; of the nature of forgiveness, not the need for revenge; of the importance of peace, not the necessity of entering the battle. How delighted they must have felt as stories were told in language they understood, using terms of reference drawn from their own experience. To be valued, understood, given time and thoughtful attention – all this must have been refreshing and inspiring. Yet we know how short a time elapsed before that same crowd reverted to old habits – calling for one to lead a rebellion, shouting and chanting for death, stirred up by each other into a frenzy of blood lust.

How difficult it is to change the attitude of a lifetime, to allow hardened hearts to soften, to receive the seeds of hope into one's soul and there nurture and encourage them. Let us pray to God for the strength to hold fast to his word, that we may fulfil his purposes for us.

Lord Jesus, let your word settle in me and bear fruit,
so that I may play a part in your harvest.

SALLY WELCH

Obstacles to healing

So many gathered around that there was no longer room for them, not even in front of the door; and he was speaking the word to them. Then some people came, bringing to him a paralysed man, carried by four of them. And when they could not bring him to Jesus because of the crowd, they removed the roof above him; and after having dug through it, they let down the mat on which the paralytic lay. When Jesus saw their faith, he said to the paralytic, 'Son, your sins are forgiven.'

What a wonderfully exciting story this is – told so simply yet with an urgency and forcefulness that serves to highlight the drama of the event. How frustrated must the friends of the paralysed man have been – having carried their burden all the way to Jesus on what must have seemed like quite an outside chance for their friend to find healing, only to discover their way blocked by the crowd. What an imaginative solution, born of desperation perhaps, but none the less effective, and how selfless of them to give up the opportunity of seeing Jesus for themselves so that their sick friend might have the opportunity of meeting him.

Here we see the crowds that surround Jesus actually preventing him, however unknowingly, from carrying out the task he came to do. Fortunately a way is found for him, and so moved is he by the faith of the group of friends that healing of body and mind is immediately forthcoming.

Sometimes it seems as if the path to mental and spiritual well-being, to living a balanced and healthy life, is so obstructed that we are unable to see the way forward clearly. Some of these obstacles may not be of our making, but there are many occasions when it is our own selves, our habits and attitudes, that stand in our way. Then we must take time to seek God's will, asking him to show us the way, confident that the path he has chosen for us will become clear.

'For surely I know the plans I have for you, says the Lord… When you search for me, you will find me' (Jeremiah 29:11–12, NRSV).

SALLY WELCH

Easily swayed

Then those who went ahead and those who followed were shouting, 'Hosanna! Blessed is the one who comes in the name of the Lord! Blessed is the coming kingdom of our ancestor David! Hosanna in the highest heaven!'... But the chief priests stirred up the crowd to have him release Barabbas for them instead.

Here it is – the ultimate, desperate irony; the demonstration of the fickle nature of the crowd which, within four short chapters, turns from hailing Jesus as their king to calling for his condemnation. Cruelly manipulated by the chief priests, the crowd unwittingly acts as an instrument of their revenge upon Jesus for the way in which he has highlighted the hypocrisy of their actions and the poverty of their faith.

It is easy to condemn the way in which this group of people can acclaim Jesus as the one who comes in the name of the Lord, only to abandon him to death a short time later. Perhaps the crowd is not the same; perhaps they fear the retribution of the temple authorities should they go against them; perhaps Barabbas is one of their own, to be preferred against the stranger from Nazareth. Whatever their motives, the result is the same and an innocent man is condemned.

The volatile nature of public opinion has been a constant theme in Jesus' life. Its power cannot be denied; its influence should not be underestimated. The courage it takes to speak out for Christ against the tide of popular beliefs and attitudes is great indeed and the voice that cries out in protest can seem very small and defenceless. The temptation to keep silent for fear of calling the wrath of the crowd upon ourselves is strong, and only those who gain their strength from God will be able to resist it.

On these occasions we can call upon the Lord to support us, and trust in his love.

'To you, O Lord, I lift up my soul. O my God, in you I trust; do not let me be put to shame; do not let my enemies exult over me. Do not let those who wait for you be put to shame' (Psalm 25:1–3a, NRSV).

SALLY WELCH

'My brother and sister'

Then his mother and his brothers came; and standing outside, they sent to him and called him. A crowd was sitting around him; and they said to him, 'Your mother and your brothers and sisters are outside, asking for you.' And he replied, 'Who are my mother and my brothers?' And looking at those who sat around him, he said, 'Here are my mother and my brothers! Whoever does the will of God is my brother and sister and mother.'

For the last two weeks, we have followed Jesus as he encounters the crowds of people who surrounded him during his ministry. Their behaviour towards him has varied, from that of engaged listening, to joyful acclamation and final condemnation. Jesus' attitude towards them, however, has never altered. He has been filled with compassion for them, taught them the ways of God, encouraged them and healed them, always acting with a deep love for every individual within the crowd and offering a permanent, open invitation to share in the kingdom. Jesus is clear-eyed about these people he loves so much – he knows that they will not understand some of this teaching, and forget even more. He is aware that his life will end in their hands, but he does not allow any of this to affect his care for them. From the very beginning of his ministry he made his position clear. The time-honoured obligations of family members towards each other have been superseded by a greater one – a relationship which includes all people, offering everyone who chooses membership of the family of God.

It is to this family that the duty of each one of us is owed also, a duty of love and care for every member, certain in the belief that in this way the kingdom of heaven will be brought closer, playing our part in its fulfilment.

My song is love unknown,
My Saviour's love to me
Love to the loveless shown
That they might lovely be.
(Samuel Crossman, 1664)

SALLY WELCH

Joel and Amos

Joel and Amos belong to the group of twelve books of the Old Testament known as the 'minor prophets' because of their relative brevity. They present history from God's perspective, pronouncing his judgement in and on history and looking forward to the day when he will usher in a new heaven and a new earth. Joel does not specify any historical details that date his prophecies, whereas Amos does, mentioning kings of Judah and Israel by name, for example.

Both prophets are clear that what mattered was speaking God's words so that people could hear and respond. Joel's opening words, 'The word of the Lord that came to Joel', and Amos' repeated 'Thus says the Lord', make it clear that God is speaking through these two servants so that their words carry divine authority. Both prophets use vivid imagery to convey their messages: locusts, a plumb-line, a basket of ripe summer fruit and, through Amos, God roars like a mighty lion. The dominant theological themes of Joel are 'the day of the Lord' and repentance, while it is the covenant that provides the backdrop for what Amos has to say. Israel had previously supposed that 'the day of the Lord' meant the time when God would defeat all her enemies and she would be exalted over them, but Joel portrays it as a day of darkness and destruction (Joel 2:1–11) and Amos reiterated that it would be a time of darkness, not light (Amos 5:18–20).

God raised up prophets like Joel and Amos to call his people back to the covenant made at Sinai through Moses. Their words continue to be relevant to Christians today as we look forward to Christ's second coming and the restoration of all creation. 2 Peter 1:19–21 reminds us that biblical prophecy comes through the words of men and women who are moved by the Holy Spirit, and we do well to be attentive to them as to a lamp shining in a dark place. The final 'day of the Lord' when the 'morning star' will rise in our hearts is still to come and, until that time, God's words stand firm, calling us to faithful living and proclamation of his word.

LIZ HOARE

Wake up and listen!

The word of the Lord that came to Joel son of Pethuel: Hear this, O elders, give ear, all inhabitants of the land! Has such a thing happened in your days, or in the days of your ancestors? Tell your children of it, and let your children tell their children, and their children another generation. What the cutting locust left, the swarming locust has eaten. What the swarming locust left, the hopping locust has eaten, and what the hopping locust left, the destroying locust has eaten. Wake up you drunkards and weep; and wail all you wine-drinkers, over the sweet wine, for it is cut off from your mouth. For a nation has invaded my land, powerful and innumerable; its teeth are lions' teeth and it has the fangs of a lioness.

Joel means 'YHWH is God' and Pethuel means 'the straightforwardness of God'; together they sum up the message of the book in that it is wholly God-focused and absolutely clear: God says judgement is coming, therefore repent and receive my blessing in the last days. Joel describes a terrible plague of locusts to indicate the nature of the impending judgement. Is it a literal swarm of insects or is it a simile for the devastation caused by an invading army? Locusts cut, swarm, hop and destroy, and recovery takes many years; the point is that it is something to instil terror on every front. It is worth remembering that this was one of the ten plagues of destruction sent on Egypt prior to the Exodus, but now it is God's own people who have suffered the devastation.

The plague is a wake-up call. Drunkards sleep and wine distracts with merry-making but now is the time to awaken and mourn. When something happens on this scale, it acts as a clarion call to stop sleep-walking into disaster and live differently. War and natural disasters do sometimes make people turn to God, especially if there are prophets who can be signposts to point the way.

What are the wake-up calls that could make the modern world turn to God in repentance and faith?

LIZ HOARE

The whole earth is groaning

Sanctify a fast, call a solemn assembly. Gather the elders and all the inhabitants of the land to the house of the Lord your God, and cry out to the Lord. Alas for the day! For the day of the Lord is near, and as destruction from the Almighty it comes. Is not the food cut off before our eyes, joy and gladness from the house of our God? The seed shrivels under the clods, the storehouses are desolate; the granaries are ruined because the grain has failed. How the animals groan! The herds of cattle wander about because there is no pasture for them; even the flocks of sheep are dazed.

Everything is affected by the approaching disaster: from the physical necessities of life like food, to the natural world on which the people depended, and inevitably to the emotional well-being of the nation. Joy and gladness have fled as the prophet cries 'Alas!' It was as if the whole world had caved in, leaving fear and insecurity everywhere, and the worst of it was that it came from the God who they expected to lead them to victory.

This is difficult to comprehend for us, as it must have been for them. It is not a simplistic way of saying that God sends every disaster, but here, at least, it arises out of the rejection of God's call on Judah to live faithfully. Joel does not spell out Judah's sin but, as Joel's name suggests, it seems likely that they had gone after other gods to worship. Joel therefore calls the people back to YHWH in repentance. The previous verse is addressed to the priests, the guardians of religious devotion, and they are bidden to put on sackcloth as a sign of repentance. This must be more than a mere show of remorse. A fast and a solemn assembly with everyone gathered at the house of the Lord to cry for mercy are commanded.

Joel's reference to creation itself being affected by the people's sin has special resonance for today. Paul wrote of the whole of creation 'groaning' (Romans 8:22). What do you think God is saying through the problems facing the natural world?

LIZ HOARE

The God of mercy and steadfast love

Yet even now, says the Lord, return to me with all your heart, with fasting, with weeping, and with mourning; rend your hearts and not your clothing. Return to the Lord your God, for he is gracious and merciful, slow to anger, and abounding in steadfast love, and relents from punishing. Who knows whether he will not turn and relent, and leave a blessing behind him, a grain-offering and a drink-offering for the Lord, your God? Blow the trumpet in Zion; sanctify a fast; call a solemn assembly; gather the people. Sanctify the congregation; assemble the aged; gather the children, even infants at the breast. Let the bridegroom leave his room and the bride her canopy.

Having described the great and terrible day of the Lord further, Joel reinforced the fact that this day would be a dreadful occasion and not something to anticipate with joy. He described an invading army who, like the locusts in chapter 1, would swarm over the land, leaving destruction everywhere.

But even now, God offers an alternative narrative if only the people will turn back to him. If we are struggling with the idea of God's anger, these words in Joel 2:13 make it clear that we are not dealing with the kind of anger attributed to the gods of the pagans. YHWH is gracious and merciful, slow to anger and abounding in steadfast love. His patience goes beyond anything humans can comprehend and his delight in mercy and loving-kindness was something that his people had experienced over and over again. When we are told that he is 'slow to anger', it is because the door to repentance and forgiveness is being held open, even when it seems that human sin has gone beyond any hope of mercy. The Lord Jesus demonstrated the lengths to which God was prepared to go to forgive and redeem the world. The mercy Joel describes here is for all, but all must be brought to a place of being willing to seek it and the need is urgent. Even suckling infants need to be covered by this mercy.

Ponder the characteristics of God described here and lean into his abundant steadfast love.

LIZ HOARE

The promise of restoration

I will repay you for the years that the swarming locust has eaten, the hopper, the destroyer, and the cutter, my great army, which I sent against you. You shall eat in plenty and be satisfied, and praise the name of the Lord your God, who has dealt wondrously with you. And my people shall never again be put to shame. You shall know that I am in the midst of Israel, and that I, the Lord, am your God and there is no other. And my people shall never again be put to shame.

This passage describes the complete reversal of the opening picture of destruction that threatened Judah. The invading army will be put to flight. Instead of famine and desolation, there will be an abundance of good things to eat. Joel described a land of fruitfulness and plenty, full barns and vats overflowing with oil and wine. The people will turn back to God and give him due praise and be able to hold their heads high, dignity replacing shame.

Many individuals have found deep comfort in the assurance that God promises to 'restore… the years which the… locust has eaten' (2:25, RSV), whatever form that 'locust' might take, but there is a larger fulfilment of this verse awaited as well. The prophet looks forward to the last days when there will never again be a threat of destruction because God himself is on the throne. Christians continue to hope in these promises of renewal and restoration of all things, the day when Christ comes to take his rightful place as Lord of the whole earth. It may seem a long time coming, but we may recall yesterday's words that the Lord is 'slow to anger and abounding in steadfast love, and relents from punishing' and be encouraged to trust that God's timing is part of his plan. Jesus calls us to watch and be ready in the meantime (Matthew 25).

'Your kingdom come.' Where do you see signs of God's renewal and restoration in the world and in your own life?

LIZ HOARE

God's Spirit poured out

Then afterwards I will pour out my spirit on all flesh; your sons and your daughters shall prophesy, your old men shall dream dreams, and your young men shall see visions. Even on the male and female slaves, in those days, I will pour out my spirit. I will show portents in the heavens and on the earth, blood and fire and columns of smoke. The sun shall be turned to darkness and the moon to blood, before the great and terrible day of the Lord comes. Then everyone who calls on the name of the Lord shall be saved; for in Mount Zion and in Jerusalem there shall be those who escape, as the Lord has said, and among the survivors shall be those whom the Lord calls.

This passage is often read at Pentecost and indeed was referred to by Peter in his Pentecost sermon in Acts 2 where he quoted Joel at length. In the Old Testament, God gave special measures of his Spirit to individuals to equip them for their calling, but Joel widens this to include all categories of people in Judah. Peter's sermon widens the scope further to apply to everyone who is a Christian. All believers are indwelt by God's Spirit, who is the mark of their belonging to Christ (see Romans 8).

To be filled with God's Spirit is to see things differently and the gifts of prophecy, dreams and visions are given to the church as gifts to build up the body of Christ. Joel did not live to see this day, but he had a message of salvation to bring to Judah nevertheless. The Holy Spirit is still at work, pouring out his blessing on you and me and all who believe. Calling on the name of the Lord goes beyond occasional religious observance, of course, for it means trusting God for the whole of life and living it in a way that honours that name.

God's promise to 'pour out' his Spirit indicates his abundant generosity. He does not stint his love and mercy but gives freely of himself to all who seek him.

LIZ HOARE

The Lord's presence is life in abundance

The Lord roars from Zion, and utters his voice from Jerusalem, and the heavens and the earth shake. But the Lord is a refuge for his people, a stronghold for the people of Israel. So you shall know that I, the Lord your God, dwell in Zion, my holy mountain. And Jerusalem shall be holy, and strangers shall never again pass through it. On that day the mountains shall drip sweet wine, the hills shall flow with milk, and all the stream beds of Judah shall flow with water; a fountain shall come forth from the house of the Lord and water the Wadi Shittim.

The power and majesty of God are not in doubt here, and the time is approaching when there will be nowhere secure to hide. But the Lord himself will shelter his vulnerable people and they will know for sure that he will be with them forever. Water in dry and desert lands means life and in the Bible it is another symbol of the Holy Spirit. Jesus taught that he was the water of life and that out of all who come to him would flow rivers of living water.

Though he began with a picture of death and destruction, Joel's final picture is of a life-giving environment where God himself dwells. It is echoed in Revelation 22 where the river of the water of life flows from the throne of God and of the Lamb through the middle of the holy city. Thus the restoration of the land and people and the deliverance of God's people on the day of judgement mean that they will know for certain that YHWH is indeed God (see 1:1). God is not and has never been a god who is far off, but the God who has made himself known. He is a relational God who looks for people to worship him. He comes to dwell with human beings and in doing so makes us holy as he is holy.

---

*In Jesus, God took flesh and 'dwelt among us' full of grace and truth
(John 1:14). Hundreds of years before, the prophet Joel testified
to this same God.*

LIZ HOARE

The prophet of God's justice

The words of Amos, who was among the shepherds of Tekoa, which he saw concerning Israel in the days of King Uzziah of Judah and in the days of King Jeroboam son of Joash of Israel, two years before the earthquake. And he said: The Lord roars from Zion, and utters his voice from Jerusalem; the pastures of the shepherds wither, and the top of Carmel dries up. Thus says the Lord: For three transgressions of Damascus, and for four, I will not revoke the punishment; because they have threshed Gilead with threshing-sledges of iron. So I will send a fire on the house of Hazael, and it shall devour the strongholds of Ben-hadad.

Tekoa was near Jerusalem in the kingdom of Judah. Amos did not consider himself a prophet, merely an ordinary man, a herdsman and a dresser of sycamore trees (see 7:14). He obeyed a call from God to utter hard and difficult-to-hear words, for Amos was not simply commenting on his own authority against the injustices that he saw around him; his words are carefully located in a historical context, for God was speaking into history through his prophet.

The image of the roaring lion is a recurring one in Amos and conjures up the awesome nature of God's power and authority. Here his roar of rage withers the pasture land and dries up Mount Carmel. The prophecy pronounced here against Damascus was followed by similar denunciations of other nations: Gaza, Tyre, Edom, the Ammonites and Moab. All had troubled the Lord's people at different times and their atrocities flew in the face of God's justice, stirring up his anger against them.

Oracles against the nations appear in many other prophetic books and are a reminder that all people everywhere are accountable to God because questions of justice, fairness and humility apply to the whole of humanity. All of us are made in the image of God and carry responsibility for our actions towards others, as Paul points out in Romans 1.

Lord God, may justice and fairness govern the hearts of the rulers of this world so that your name is honoured. Amen

LIZ HOARE

Great privilege brings great responsibility for God's people

Thus says the Lord: For three transgressions of Judah, and for four, I will not revoke the punishment; because they have rejected the law of the Lord, and have not kept his statutes, but they have been led astray by the same lies after which their ancestors walked. So I will send a fire on Judah and it shall devour the strongholds of Jerusalem. Thus says the Lord: For three transgressions of Israel, and for four, I will not revoke the punishment; because they sell the righteous for silver, and the needy for a pair of sandals – they who trample the head of the poor into the dust of the earth, and push the afflicted out of the way; father and son go in to the same girl, so that my holy name is profaned; they lay themselves down beside every altar on garments taken in pledge; and in the house of their God they drink wine bought with the fines they imposed.

If we can imagine the satisfaction Israel felt listening to Amos' denunciations of the foreign nations that had treated her unjustly, we may imagine the delicious sense of vindication as the lion roared against her close neighbour Judah. But imagine the total shock as the prophet turned his roar to condemn Israel itself for its own unfaithfulness. Amos reserves his most fierce condemnation for God's people, who bore a special responsibility to live holy lives because of their particular relationship to God. Both Judah and Israel had rejected God's law, taken to idolatry and abandoned compassion and kindness, the very qualities that God had revealed to them as the heart of his own character. In particular, their disregard for the poor and needy, the way they cheated them and trampled on them are set alongside their immorality and idolatry. Israel had become just like all the other nations and so their sins were her sins also, but because of their special relationship to God, his judgement fell on them all the more fiercely. The passage shows us what angers God and how inseparable right worship is from right behaviour.

Lord, may we who profess your name live lives
that commend your character. Amen

LIZ HOARE

The Lord's lament for his people

Hear this word that the Lord has spoken against you, O people of Israel, against the whole family that I brought up out of the land of Egypt: You only have I known of all the families of the earth; therefore I will punish you for all your iniquities. Do two walk together unless they have made an appointment? Does a lion roar in the forest, when it has no prey? Does a young lion cry out from its den, if it has caught nothing? Does a bird fall into a snare on the earth, when there is no trap for it? Does a snare spring up from the ground, when it has taken nothing? Is a trumpet blown in a city, and the people are not afraid? Does disaster befall a city, unless the Lord has done it? Surely the Lord does nothing, without revealing his secrets to his servants the prophets. The lion has roared; who will not fear? The Lord has spoken; who can but prophesy?

History, creation and the word of the Lord tell the same story here. Israel is summoned to hear the judgement the Lord has spoken against them (3:1). We can detect God's heartache in his lament at this perfidious betrayal of his love, forcing him to denounce the very people he had chosen as his own. Reference to the pivotal moment in Israel's history when God rescued them from Egypt makes clear the fairness of his judgement. The word 'known' in verse 2 is the same as that in Genesis 4:1 where it is used of Adam and Eve, implying deep intimate knowing. What a privilege!

But Israel was not chosen simply for the privileges that would come her way. With election came the responsibility to be God's witnesses in the world. The evidence was against her but, even now, the images of the lion's roar and the trumpet blast carry in them a call to repent. A further sign of God's just nature is his insistence that he will not act in judgement without first revealing his secrets to his prophets.

How does the picture of God yearning for his people in this passage speak to you?

LIZ HOARE

God says, 'Seek me and live'

Therefore, thus I will do to you, O Israel; because I will do this to you, prepare to meet your God, O Israel! For lo, the one who forms the mountains, creates the wind, reveals his thoughts to mortals, makes the morning darkness, and treads on the heights of the earth – the Lord, the God of hosts, is his name! Hear this word that I take up over you in lamentation, O house of Israel: Fallen, no more to rise, is maiden Israel; forsaken on her land, with no one to raise her up. For thus says the Lord God: The city that marched out a thousand shall have a hundred left and that which marched out a hundred shall have ten left. For thus says the Lord to the house of Israel: Seek me and live.

'Prepare to meet your God' is a favourite of those who put up placards with Bible verses on them, usually designed to frighten people into obedience to God's commandments. But who is this God we are being threatened with, and can we, in fact, be put into a right relationship with him through fear?

There are some helpful indications in this brief passage of God's character: he is not a tyrannical deity demanding our cowering obeisance. He is the creator who formed the world and rules over it (4:13). He is powerful, yes, for 'the Lord, the God of hosts, is his name' (4:13), but he reaches out to his creatures in intimacy as he reveals his thoughts to human beings (5:1). He is therefore relational in his dealings with men and women and when we do not listen he laments over us in grief (5:1). No other deity was ever portrayed like this. Even as he pronounces judgement, he holds out the way back to that life-giving relationship with him, for as he warns of the false way he pleads, 'Seek me and live.'

'Perfect love casts out fear' (1 John 4:18). What image of God do you hold in your heart as you come into his presence today?

LIZ HOARE

Let justice roll down like waters

Seek good and not evil, that you may live; and so the Lord, the God of hosts, will be with you, just as you have said. Hate evil and love good, and establish justice in the gate; it may be that the Lord, the God of hosts, will be gracious to the remnant of Joseph… I hate, I despise your festivals, and I take no delight in your solemn assemblies. Even though you offer me your burnt-offerings and grain-offerings, I will not accept them; and the offerings of well-being of your fatted animals I will not look upon. Take away from me the noise of your songs; I will not listen to the melody of your harps. But let justice roll down like waters, and righteousness like an ever-flowing stream.

Love and hate are two passionate emotions that leave no room for compromise. 'I will not accept them' in verse 22 literally means 'I will not smell them'. This, added to 'I will not look upon' and 'I will not listen', vividly portray the total disgust of God towards empty worship and unjust actions. Complacency and compromise dishonour our passionate God, who looks for goodness in the form of justice and righteousness, and who despises worship that is elaborate and meticulous on the outside but empty at its heart. A church that does not pay heed to this will die. Revelation 3:15–16 describes a church rejected because it is neither cold nor hot, but merely lukewarm.

The Lord Jesus has shown us what true goodness looks like and his passion for the truth took him to the cross. We cannot redefine goodness on any other terms without betraying the Lord himself, who is at the heart of our faith. Ponder what God hates and what he looks for in his people in the church today. What does it mean to respond to seek good rather than evil and so find life? Where does justice need to roll down like waters in our society?

Pray for your church, that it will offer Christ-centred worship that spills over into daily Christ-filled lives that actively seek good and hate evil.

LIZ HOARE

The cost of faithful witness

Then Amaziah, the priest of Bethel, sent to King Jeroboam of Israel, saying, 'Amos has conspired against you in the very centre of the house of Israel; the land is not able to bear all his words. For thus Amos has said, "Jeroboam shall die by the sword, and Israel must go into exile away from his land."' And Amaziah said to Amos, 'O seer, go, flee away to the land of Judah, earn your bread there, and prophesy there; but never again prophesy at Bethel, for it is the king's sanctuary, and it is a temple of the kingdom.'

The context of this fierce opposition to Amos' prophetic ministry is yet another denunciation of Israel. A vivid image, a plumb-line, has been used to show failure to measure up to God's expectations and the pronouncement of the destruction of the high places, the sanctuaries and even the royal house itself. Amaziah the priest repeats Amos' words to the king and tries to force the prophet to go home, back to Judah where he belonged and where he could trouble Israel no longer. Amaziah refused to acknowledge the authority of Amos' prophetic words as being of God.

Here, king and priest are pitted against the prophet. In Jesus, the living Word of God, we are shown prophet, priest and king in one true unity. Meanwhile, Amos refused to be silenced and went on to present a further vivid image, this time of a basket of summer fruit signifying the final end of Israel as a nation. Like the fruit, she is ripe for judgement. Imagine how hard it must have been for Amos to persevere not only in the face of such opposition and rejection, but also in the cost of speaking these harsh words of condemnation and destruction. It was a difficult calling and a far cry from tending figs and herding sheep.

Reflect on the way many of God's Christian people who would have settled for a quiet life, instead responded to his claim on them and followed faithfully where he led, trusting in Jesus, their prophet, priest and true king. Pray for Christians under persecution around the world.

LIZ HOARE

A severe warning

On that day, says the Lord God, I will make the sun go down at noon, and darken the earth in broad daylight. I will turn your feasts into mourning, and all your songs into lamentation; I will bring sackcloth on all loins, and baldness on every head; I will make it like the mourning for an only son, and the end of it like a bitter day. The time is surely coming, says the Lord God, when I will send a famine on the land; not a famine of bread, or a thirst for water, but of hearing the words of the Lord. They shall wander from sea to sea, and from north to east; they shall run to and fro, seeking the word of the Lord, but they shall not find it.

These fearful words of reversal are startling and disorientating. The Old Testament prophets frequently turn to the natural world to illustrate the impact of God's word to human beings. Here portents in the sky turn day into night and cause confusion, while merriment and celebration changes to grief and lamentation. With perhaps an allusion to the bitterness of the Egyptians at the time of the Exodus, with the loss of their firstborn, God highlights the depth of the grief to come.

At last the people turn to God, but they will not find him. Like someone blindly running first in one direction and then in another looking for they know not what, so will God's people be as they realise what they have lost. What bitter irony that God's people, who had repeatedly ignored his words calling them to repentance and right living, now discover he is no longer speaking to them. These words of Amos are a sober reminder that, though God is infinitely patient, we may grow so deaf to his mercy that we cannot hear him any more. How do you think that plays out in our own time?

In your prayer time, ponder the way that Jesus came to his own and his own did not receive him. Ask God to open deaf ears today so that the living Word may be heard and received.

LIZ HOARE

God renews his covenant

The eyes of the Lord are upon the sinful kingdom, and I will destroy it from the face of the earth – except that I will not utterly destroy the house of Jacob, says the Lord… On that day I will raise up the booth of David that is fallen, and repair its breaches, and raise up its ruins, and rebuild it as in the days of old; in order that they may possess the remnant of Edom and all the nations who are called by name, says the Lord who does this… I will restore the fortunes of my people Israel, and they shall rebuild the ruined cities and inhabit them; they shall plant vineyards and drink their wine, and they shall make gardens and eat their fruit.

Amos ends on a note of hope, even though judgement is assuredly coming. In 721BC the northern kingdom was wiped off the pages of history when Assyria conquered Israel and carried her people away into exile. But this is not God's final word, and Amos ends with an oracle of restoration.

So what has all the vigorous denunciation of wickedness been about? Is God giving in and saying it doesn't matter? Amos is clear that justice and righteousness are God's very nature and the focus has been on the consistency of his character throughout. He is not changing his mind, but rather reaffirming his love and commitment to his covenant of grace. In saving a remnant of 'the house of Jacob' God's covenant will be renewed and brought to fulfilment. There is no going back. But anyone who truly seeks after God will live, as Amos has made clear elsewhere. God's faithfulness has been stressed again and again. Now Amos describes the restoration of his people with beautiful imagery of fruitfulness and all the security it implies. There is a hint in verse 12 that God's mercy extends far beyond the confines of his chosen nation too. As the New Testament affirms, God will complete his purposes in history and renew the whole creation.

Our readings in Amos end in hope purely because of God's mercy and loving kindness. Reflect on what you have learned about God's character through his faithful prophet.

LIZ HOARE

Discipleship

Traditionally, the word 'disciple' has conjured up images of a bunch of bearded men in robes and sandals walking a dusty Middle Eastern road. You may recall the classic Christian book *Discipleship* by the late David Watson – and I confess that the title was on my 'ought-to-read' list for years, but somehow I never quite got round to it. 'Discipleship' and being a 'disciple' can sound a bit worthy and old-fashioned, hardly concepts to pull in the crowds.

When we turn to the New Testament epistles, we find that the task of turning new believers into disciples – dedicated followers of the Lord – was what absorbed most of the energy of the apostles. Churches were springing up across Greece and Asia Minor as expressions of a radically different way of living. Men and women were choosing – often at great personal cost – to align themselves with a kingdom that did not adhere to the barren values of the Roman Empire.

These brave new believers needed nurturing in the faith, instruction on what it meant to belong together and advice on how they should conduct themselves as a community. This was all encompassed by the idea of 'discipleship'. Far from implying some kind of moral worthiness or old-fashioned sensibility, being a disciple meant boldly identifying as counter-cultural, embodying (individually and also collectively) Christ himself.

Over the next fortnight, we will explore some of the epistles' teaching on discipleship, both for the individual believer and for the local church. Despite more than two millennia separating those first disciples from us today, we face remarkably similar challenges as we work out what it means to follow Christ. Many of the epistles were addressed to churches in busy urban centres, where members had to deal with commercial, philosophical and social pressures not unrecognisable to readers in 2018.

Like those first Christians, we need to know what we believe – and why. Like them, we need to explore the implications of what we believe for every area of our lives. And, like them, we have to keep our focus on the 'main thing' – 'the testimony about God... Jesus Christ and him crucified', in the words of Paul to one of his more troublesome congregations (1 Corinthians 2:1–2, NIV).

NAOMI STARKEY

Challenge to holiness

Therefore, since we have such a hope, we are very bold. We are not like Moses, who would put a veil over his face to prevent the Israelites from seeing the end of what was passing away… But whenever anyone turns to the Lord, the veil is taken away. Now the Lord is the Spirit, and where the Spirit of the Lord is, there is freedom. And we all, who with unveiled faces contemplate the Lord's glory, are being transformed into his image with ever-increasing glory, which comes from the Lord, who is the Spirit.

The 'hope' to which Paul refers here is the new covenant, the 'ministry of the Spirit' (v. 8). This covenant, through its transformative power, promises life in glorious fullness where the old covenant, the 'ministry… engraved in letters on stone' (v. 7) effected by Moses, simply showed the extent to which people fell short.

The challenge here is clear: turning to the Lord means facing up to our need for transformation, a need which becomes blindingly obvious the more we allow the light of God's glory into our lives. Thanks to the hope of the new covenant, however, this need is not a cause for despair. When we come to God as we are, with all our shabby shortcomings, the miracle of grace occurs. It is as if a veil is removed from our faces and we are revealed as we truly are: not stumbling sinners, but children of the light. Thanks to the salvation won for us by Christ, we are – astonishingly – radiant with God's glory, even as the process of transformation continues.

We hear the challenge to holiness that reverberates through scripture and we can respond with boldness, in freedom. We are freed from fear of failure because our failures have been forgiven already. As long as we continue to walk with God, as long as we allow his light to shine into every corner of our hearts, we will find his glory burning ever brighter in and through us. Like Jesus our Lord and brother, we can become lights to the world (Matthew 5:14).

Spirit of God, I pray that heaven's glory may burn brighter in me today.

NAOMI STARKEY

Challenge to persevere

Therefore we do not lose heart. Though outwardly we are wasting away, yet inwardly we are being renewed day by day. For our light and momentary troubles are achieving for us an eternal glory that far outweighs them all. So we fix our eyes not on what is seen, but on what is unseen, since what is seen is temporary, but what is unseen is eternal. For we know that if the earthly tent we live in is destroyed, we have a building from God, an eternal house in heaven, not built by human hands.

In this passage Paul writes with beautiful eloquence, yet with such a depth of challenge. Never one for soothing platitudes, he nevertheless demonstrates pastoral sensitivity while reminding the Corinthian congregation of the 'big picture' of faith. Yes, they face troubles; yes, they are 'wasting away' – but this life is not all there is. They may lose many of their securities – social, economic, physical – but they still have the hope of an eternal home. And it is this hope that helps to sustain them, that helps them to persevere even when life feels unbearably hard.

There is a balance to be struck between 'mindful' focus on the present moment and stepping back to gain wider perspective. Job's so-called comforters failed to help their friend because they could not bear his present suffering. They found it safer to search for fault in the situation rather than stay with him in his pain ('Do not despise the discipline of the Almighty,' says Eliphaz the Temanite unhelpfully, in Job 5:17). Paul acknowledges the difficulties both he and the young Christians face – but reminds them (and himself) that outward, temporal troubles are more than counter-balanced by inner, eternal truths.

This is not a call to escapism, tempting though that might be. Paul issues a challenge to his congregation to persevere because of the eternal hope they share, but also because the troubles are themselves a means of grace; God's way of renewal until 'eternal glory' is achieved. Persevere, step by step, day by day – because the only way is through.

Hold before God any whom you know (including yourself, perhaps) who need the gift of perseverance today.

NAOMI STARKEY

Challenge to humility

Do nothing out of selfish ambition or vain conceit. Rather, in humility value others above yourselves, not looking to your own interests but each of you to the interests of the others. In your relationships with one another, have the same mindset as Christ Jesus: who, being in very nature God, did not consider equality with God something to be used to his own advantage; rather, he made himself nothing by taking the very nature of a servant, being made in human likeness. And being found in appearance as a man, he humbled himself by becoming obedient to death – even death on a cross!

I find it enlightening to remember that the justifiably famous 'Christ-hymn' of vv. 6–11 concludes an exhortation to humility for 'God's holy people in Christ Jesus at Philippi' (1:1). Paul pretty much bursts into song about the person and divinity of Jesus, not simply for doctrinal clarity but as a way of spelling out to his audience the 'mindset' expected of them.

He is making a forceful point (as always!) that involves one of the building blocks of healthy church communities.

Membership is emphatically not about personal status; it is about servanthood. And this servanthood is not false modesty; it is about consciously setting aside any status you happen to possess, through birth, education, work or anything else. This is what Jesus did, says Paul, and so you, his followers, must do likewise. It is a message so deceptively straightforward to hear, yet potentially so difficult to put into practice. Furthermore, this is a message for everyone, for leaders as well as members, for those on the preaching team as well as those on the coffee rota.

Such a message of mutual submission and care resonates through Paul's writings, including teaching on marriage (Ephesians 5:21–33). Living this way can feel a challenge too far – who will look out for my interests if I don't? 'Your brothers and sisters in Christ' is Paul's uncompromising answer.

Picture your church congregation – or, if you belong to a large church, those members whom you know well. Then ask God to show you how you can demonstrate in that congregation the same 'mindset' as Jesus.

NAOMI STARKEY

Challenge to discipline

Do you not know that in a race all the runners run, but only one gets the prize? Run in such a way as to get the prize. Everyone who competes in the games goes into strict training. They do it to get a crown that will not last, but we do it to get a crown that will last forever. Therefore I do not run like someone running aimlessly; I do not fight like a boxer beating the air. No, I strike a blow to my body and make it my slave so that after I have preached to others, I myself will not be disqualified for the prize.

The quiet lanes of the Llyn Peninsula, where I currently live, are ideal for running. I have learned how the right mental attitude helps to keep me going: persevering (as we reflected earlier this week), rather than anticipating too vividly the finish when still at the start of a 10-mile slog. As Paul reflects here, however, perseverance must be combined with the discipline of training to be truly effective. I may harbour dreams of running a marathon, but dreams are unlikely to become reality without training. Positive thinking and determination are not enough when the legs pack up, unused to going quite so far!

We may feel that Paul's attitude to the body sounds too harsh – surely Christians shouldn't have a 'mortifying the flesh' reputation? If you are a serious Olympic athlete, though, you can't afford to relax your arduous regime, even in holiday season. You have to sacrifice leisure and family time, and submit to lifestyle restrictions that most people wouldn't countenance, in order to keep your medal hopes alive. That kind of discipline is what Paul is referring to, writing to a community in a city that hosted the Isthmian (similar to the Olympic) Games every other year.

As ever, Paul practises what he preaches. He does not prescribe to others what he does not do himself. That kind of mental vigilance is a particular discipline that those in leadership positions would do well to cultivate.

Lord God, we pray that you will give us the discipline
to become spiritually fit and focused for you.

NAOMI STARKEY

Challenge to fruitfulness

But the fruit of the Spirit is love, joy, peace, forbearance, kindness, goodness, faithfulness, gentleness and self-control. Against such things there is no law. Those who belong to Christ Jesus have crucified the flesh with its passions and desires. Since we live by the Spirit, let us keep in step with the Spirit. Let us not become conceited, provoking and envying each other.

These much-quoted verses come at the end of a section where Paul is exhorting his 'brothers and sisters' in the churches of Galatia (a Roman province in present-day central Turkey). They are to celebrate the freedom won for them by Christ (5:1), while not abusing that freedom by indulging 'the flesh' (v. 13). Paul provides a list of 'the acts of the flesh' (vv. 19–21) to contrast with the 'fruit of the Spirit'. So far, so much the content of rather too many sermons that leave congregation members slinking away, mentally quantifying exactly how unfruitful they are.

Take another look: Paul is talking about the 'fruit of the Spirit', which is not something that we can produce ourselves, however hard we try. That's the bad news; the mind-blowingly good news is that the Spirit's work produces this fruit, irrespective of any human or divine law. The struggle against unholy 'passions and desires' has been conclusively won by our decision to give ourselves to Christ. All we have to do now is 'keep in step with the Spirit' – we might say 'keep up with the Spirit'. The Lord goes ahead of us; we are called to follow and receive (not strive for) the gifts and blessings that he would bring to birth in us.

The rebuke in the final verse is thus shown in context: we have no grounds for conceit or envy because we cannot boast in the fruitfulness of our lives. All we should do is give thanks to God for his generosity. The challenge remains of opening ourselves to this generosity rather than trying to hold back some little corner of ourselves from its transformative power.

'Love, joy, peace, forbearance, kindness, goodness, faithfulness, gentleness and self-control': Spirit of God, be at work to form such fruit within me.

NAOMI STARKEY

Challenge to freedom

Since you died with Christ to the elemental spiritual forces of this world, why, as though you still belonged to the world, do you submit to its rules: 'Do not handle! Do not taste! Do not touch!'? These rules, which have to do with things that are all destined to perish with use, are based on merely human commands and teachings… Since, then, you have been raised with Christ, set your hearts on things above, where Christ is, seated at the right hand of God. Set your minds on things above, not on earthly things. For you died, and your life is now hidden with Christ in God.

Death recurs often in Paul's writings as a metaphor for the dramatic division between the old life constrained by sin and failure, and the new, which is 'hidden with Christ in God.' He speaks earlier in this chapter about how reality is 'found in Christ' (v. 17) in contrast to the 'human commands and teachings', mere 'shadow of things that were to come' that can, even so, lead to men and women condemning one another. We have been born again to a life freed from such rules, which is (as Paul goes on to show) no passport to libertarianism but licence for confident discipleship.

By contrast, the institutional church (in its varied manifestations around the world) often seems to devote its energies almost exclusively to safeguarding a multiplicity of rules. What would Paul say about that? And what would Jesus say – or do? To be honest, those are unanswerable questions, but questions worth raising to jolt us from unthinking acceptance of 'the way things are'.

Paul challenges us as individual believers to seek constantly to realise the full measure of the freedom that we have in Christ. We are, every one of us, forgiven in Christ – we are reborn, clothed in righteousness – and now we walk on, if we so choose, in the dazzling light of his grace. This is the truth (and not our helpless failures and fallings-short) that must be foundational for all institutional expressions of our faith.

---

*Startle me, Lord, with a deeper awareness of the full freedom
that you have bought for me.*

NAOMI STARKEY

Challenge to be ready

Now, brothers and sisters, about times and dates we do not need to write to you, for you know very well that the day of the Lord will come like a thief in the night… But you, brothers and sisters, are not in darkness so that this day should surprise you like a thief. You are all children of the light and children of the day. We do not belong to the night or to the darkness… Since we belong to the day, let us be sober, putting on faith and love as a breastplate, and the hope of salvation as a helmet.

Advent is the season of the church's year when attention traditionally turns to Christ's second coming and the signs thereof, by way of wider perspective on his first coming, celebrated at Christmas. Here, we have the reminder that we should be *constantly* aware of this promised return. We are to be ready and watchful, so as not to be taken by surprise.

Down the centuries, more than a few have taken this as indication that they should retreat to the hills with enough tinned food, bottled water and ammunition to survive the coming tribulation. Whether or not that particular scenario tempts us, we must all wait for the 'day of the Lord' – and we wait… and still we wait, as so many have waited for so many centuries, holding to scripture's assertion that 'only the Father' knows exactly when that day will be (Matthew 24:36–42; Mark 13:32–37).

How should we conduct ourselves, meanwhile? We must make ourselves ready, Paul says, by never forgetting that we are 'children of the light and children of the day' – and by living accordingly. We need the protection afforded by faith and love, and our hope of salvation should always be to hand, further spiritual armour to protect us against attack. And we should remind ourselves – and one another – that as disciples of Christ, we are part of a greater narrative, a longer story, than is encompassed by our individual lifespan.

Show me, Lord God, what I should do this day, to make sure that I am ready for the day of your coming, whenever that may be.

NAOMI STARKEY

Belonging together

Just as a body, though one, has many parts, but all its many parts form one body, so it is with Christ. For we were all baptised by one Spirit so as to form one body – whether Jews or Gentiles, slave or free – and we were all given the one Spirit to drink. Even so the body is not made up of one part but of many... Now you are the body of Christ, and each one of you is a part of it.

In our second week reflecting on discipleship, we will focus on growing together as followers of Jesus. It is easy for churches to get caught up with cash flow or headcount or simply 'keeping the show on the road', so that the whole idea of discipleship gets sidelined. Yet building up each other's faith, learning about prayer and reflecting on scripture together are as crucial to being a healthy and growing community as attending Sunday worship.

It is poignant to read this section of 1 Corinthians in the light of the centuries since it was penned. Far from being 'one body', humanity has all too often usurped church authority and made it another method of political control. Agreeing to disagree about what are often (let's be honest) secondary issues is just about tolerable. What history has shown us, however, is matters of faith regularly used to humiliate, if not destroy, the 'opposition', whoever they might be.

Let's return to the basics: as the Lord's disciples, we are a body; we belong together. As time passes, some parts of the body may cause pain to others; some parts may be in need of treatment, but it is surely better to work towards healing rather than amputation. There is so much more that unites than divides us, but it is easy to forget or ignore that. Of course there is difference; the trouble starts when no attempt is made to accommodate or even tolerate difference.

'We are the body of Christ. In the one Spirit we were all baptised into one body. Let us pursue all that makes for peace and builds up our common life.' (From the Anglican service of Holy Communion)

NAOMI STARKEY

Worshipping together

Follow the way of love and eagerly desire gifts of the Spirit, especially prophecy. For anyone who speaks in a tongue does not speak to people but to God. Indeed, no one understands them; they utter mysteries by the Spirit. But the one who prophesies speaks to people for their strengthening, encouraging and comfort... I would like every one of you to speak in tongues, but I would rather have you prophesy. The one who prophesies is greater than the one who speaks in tongues, unless someone interprets, so that the church may be edified.

Some parts of the church have considered speaking in 'tongues' the definitive mark of true discipleship. People report feeling so overcome by God's love that they are literally moved beyond words and break into praise using an unknown language. A friend told me of how, as a very young Christian, he felt so pressurised to manifest this gift that he ended up saying the Lord's Prayer in Welsh (a language he spoke anyway) as a get-out. The kind but unknowing team praying over him were delighted!

Paul provides a helpful context for this and similar spiritual gifts. He rates prophecy above 'tongues', since this gift can edify the rest of the congregation. We should note, by the way, that prophecy means not so much 'predicting the future' as 'telling it like it really is' – spelling out the likely consequences of certain behaviours or courses of action (as did so many Old Testament prophets). Worship, then, is something to share together, a way of uniting the body of Christ, and not a bunch of individuals, each locked into a personal experience. Those who are leading worship have to be conscious always of inclusion, of enabling as far as possible everybody to participate on equal terms.

What is clearly important, too, is that worshipping congregations understand what is going on. This is true whether or not a church is ritual-heavy or self-consciously going against any kind of formality. As we worship together, we journey together to meet the God who is both eternal mystery and incarnate Word.

Pray for your local church, especially for those leading the worship, and ask God's Holy Spirit to enrich and enliven the next time you gather.

NAOMI STARKEY

Nurture together

Each of you must put off falsehood... Anyone who has been stealing must steal no longer, but must work... that they may have something to share with those in need. Do not let any unwholesome talk come out of your mouths, but only what is helpful for building others up... And do not grieve the Holy Spirit of God, with whom you were sealed for the day of redemption. Get rid of all bitterness, rage and anger, brawling and slander, along with every form of malice. Be kind and compassionate to one another, forgiving each other, just as in Christ God forgave you.

How easy it is to develop a hierarchy of transgressions, without even being aware of it! We would agree that stealing is reprehensible (not to say criminal), although mercy may be extended if the thief is in desperate need. Rage, anger, brawling and outright slander are not usually condoned. But how bad is bitterness? Are there grounds for an occasional politic falsehood (nothing as clumsy as a lie)? And what exactly is 'unwholesome talk'?

This passage does not simply list wrongful behaviours and attitudes; it provides a timely reminder of the context to which we belong as disciples. And this context vastly transcends our limited perspectives and biased and self-justifying judgements. In our dealings with one another, we are to follow the example of Christ himself. We don't just forgive and show compassion to those we like; we are called to imitate the mercy of the Father who gave his own Son for us, even before we knew our need for mercy.

That unbelievably bold summons to godly living indicates the costliness of the 'kindness and compassion' we are urged to show. We are not called to demonstrate a kind of bland niceness but a depth of nurturing care that we cannot hope to produce on our own. We need the Spirit of God to grow it within us. That same Spirit will be grieved by our mistreatment of others – whether that mistreatment happens face-to-face or in more subtle, yet potentially no less damaging ways.

Lord, teach us to care for one another – and enlarge our hearts
to nurture one another as tenderly as you nurture us.

NAOMI STARKEY

Learn together

We always thank God… when we pray for you, because we have heard of your faith in Christ Jesus and of the love you have for all God's people – the faith and love that spring from the hope stored up for you in heaven and about which you have already heard in the true message of the gospel that has come to you. In the same way, the gospel is bearing fruit and growing throughout the whole world – just as it has been doing among you since the day you heard it and truly understood God's grace.

The early church can sound so exciting to us – yet it was also precarious. I find it hard to imagine the challenge of passing on the faith without recourse to a New Testament, let alone formal creeds, respected theologians or a single Christian paperback! In some ways, the simplicity sounds beguiling, but a glance at the epistles shows how Paul, for one, had to spend a great deal of time and heartache safeguarding the message passed on to the new congregations. Errors, misinterpretations and unhelpful emphases flourished back then as much as they flourish now.

What we see in those early years is a process that we need to continue now: the process of learning together, deepening our understanding and challenging assumptions while listening respectfully to each other's differing views. We are blessed with an unbelievable wealth of teaching from a myriad of traditions to guide us. Certainly in the English language, we can choose from an abundance of Bible translations, in a huge variety of literary styles, to help our learning.

Our lived experience of the gospel is crucial, but so is testing those experiences against the insights of others, whether revered teachers of the faith accessed through their writings, or through discussion with our home group. Hearing but also 'truly understanding' the gospel message is linked directly with its bearing fruit and continuing to spread – learning can in no way be described as optional for disciples of Jesus.

Reflect on your church community: how do you learn together and how effective is that learning process? What could you do to encourage a stronger culture of learning?

NAOMI STARKEY

Give together

Remember this: whoever sows sparingly will also reap sparingly, and whoever sows generously will also reap generously. Each of you should give what you have decided in your heart to give, not reluctantly or under compulsion, for God loves a cheerful giver. And God is able to bless you abundantly, so that in all things at all times, having all that you need, you will abound in every good work… You will be enriched in every way so that you can be generous on every occasion, and through us your generosity will result in thanksgiving to God.

Along with music, money is probably one of the most potentially vexatious areas of church life. Whether a congregation's turnover rivals that of a highly profitable business or whether it's a matter of a hard-pressed warden reckoning the weekly offering in a handful of coins, money – or the lack of it – can exercise an overwhelming influence on church priorities.

One of the most beneficial results of recent structural reorganisation in the church in Wales, where I minister, has been a greater openness between churches about their finances. I have attended meetings where, for the first time, treasurers have disclosed their assets and debated how much their congregation can give to what is now called the Bishop's Ministry Fund (no more talk of 'quotas' or 'common fund'). The aim is to cultivate a spirit of generosity rather than 'giving as little as we can get away with' – a spirit in line with Paul's words to the Corinthians here.

Generosity blesses us because, in being generous, we focus on what we have instead of what we lack. We look at our riches instead of despair at our (relative) poverty. People visiting impoverished parts of the world report of being humbled by the generosity they encounter from those to whom they came to give. Giving – when the gift is offered freely without any kind of strings attached – bestows dignity on the giver, as well as benefiting the one who receives.

The common perception of church life is a constant round of fundraising to make ends meet. Reflect on your church – how accurate is that perception and how could it be changed?

NAOMI STARKEY

Standing together

Whatever happens, conduct yourselves in a manner worthy of the gospel of Christ. Then, whether I come and see you or only hear about you in my absence, I will know that you stand firm in the one Spirit, striving together as one for the faith of the gospel without being frightened in any way by those who oppose you... It has been granted to you on behalf of Christ not only to believe in him, but also to suffer for him, since you are going through the same struggle you saw I had.

Outright opposition can be easier to endure than indifference. Hostile regimes intending to crush the church have found that persecution actually seems to strengthen faith. There is no room for a 'take it or leave it' attitude when belief is a matter of life or death. That is the context for Paul's seemingly shocking attitude that struggle and suffering are some kind of privilege 'granted' to believers. They will struggle as he has struggled; they will suffer for Christ, although their suffering will always pale into comparison with what Christ endured for their sake.

That doesn't mean that Christians should pray for persecution. Paul is not asking the Philippian church to look for potential martyrs and encourage them to sacrifice themselves. Persecution is not glorified, but it is accepted as likely, if not inevitable. When it comes, it should be met not with aggression but with courage and steadfastness – and unity. Instead of scattering in fear, they are to hold together, stand together, and be 'worthy of the gospel of Christ'.

In many parts of the world, though, the threat to faith is not active hostility but indifference. Dwindling, ageing churches are viewed as harmless irrelevances. But we shouldn't take this as inducement to seek out opposition – 'we matter enough for others to hate us!' Instead we should give thanks for our privilege of religious freedom and pray, fervently and frequently, for our brothers and sisters elsewhere in the world who may be called to pay for their beliefs with their lives.

With your church, if you can, find out more about a country where the church is under pressure and commit yourselves to supporting in some way the Christians there.

NAOMI STARKEY

Loving together

Therefore, as God's chosen people, holy and dearly loved, clothe yourselves with compassion, kindness, humility, gentleness and patience. Bear with each other and forgive one another if any of you has a grievance against someone. Forgive as the Lord forgave you. And over all these virtues put on love, which binds them all together in perfect unity. Let the peace of Christ rule in your hearts, since as members of one body you were called to peace. And be thankful.

Here is the template for the people of God, for the local church: a group of people, 'one body', characterised by a quality of care, love and support that surpasses that shown by any other gathering. Grievances are not ignored but forgiven; knowing they are loved and already holy in their Father's eyes, church members are released to love one another.

Sadly, it can be easy for a local church to give lip service to such beautiful words. It can be easy to find excuses to shy away from the gospel challenge to build genuinely inclusive communities, and retreat instead to a self-selecting group of like-minded people. While the eclectic congregation – a church consisting not of those living closest but those who like that style of worship, preaching or whatever – is common in bigger towns and cities, this model of church can facilitate avoiding difference, whether theological or social.

In rural contexts, where church choice may well be limited to the 'local', the challenge is to build a sense of belonging with a bunch of widely (not to say wildly) diverse individuals. While this can be far from straightforward, when it does happen, it can be a powerful witness. As a cleric once commented to me, the church was the one group in his village where members were able to coexist and work together, despite occasional fallings-out. Faulty and frail as congregation members were (as we all are), they knew that what united them was stronger and more important than what might drive them apart.

Heavenly Father, bless my church with compassion, kindness, humility, gentleness and patience. May we experience the depth of your forgiveness, so that we truly forgive each other.

NAOMI STARKEY

Jerusalem

The Bible is a Holy Land guide in a double sense: it explains why some places in the Middle East are so significant within world history, and also how that history points beyond itself to the place of ultimate holiness and beauty we call heaven. In this series, we find inspiration by taking a tour through the biblical record about Jerusalem and past that record towards 'the city of the living God, the heavenly Jerusalem' (Hebrews 12:22).

The holy city of Jerusalem, built as a city that is bound firmly together by Jewish King David (Psalm 122:3), is central to the revelation of God in Jesus Christ, although its unity is qualified. In this fortnight's Lenten readings, which parallel our Christian pilgrimage towards Easter, we trace Jerusalem's role in the biblical record of God's salvation gift in the intersection of time with eternity affected there through Easter and Pentecost.

Christians reread the Old Testament in the light of Christ's resurrection and the gift of the Holy Spirit, so that Jerusalem becomes a mirror of humanity in its beauty and fragility, a pointer to holiness and the need to repent. In Christian believing, it is a foretaste of the ultimate holiness and beauty found in the holy city Jerusalem coming down out of heaven from God (Revelation 21:10b).

I have been to Jerusalem and have wept there as Jesus did, wept at the miracle of love covering the multitude of our sins; but Jerusalem is yours even if you've never been to the Holy Land. The Bible will take you to Jerusalem as you allow the Holy Spirit's leading. It will secure you in God's love and build aspiration for the fulfilment of your life beyond this earthly pilgrimage.

'Come, let us go up to the mountain of the Lord, to the house of the God of Jacob; that he may teach us his ways and that we may walk in his paths. For out of Zion shall go forth instruction, and the word of the Lord from Jerusalem' (Micah 4:2).

JOHN TWISLETON

Rejoice Jerusalem!

I asked, 'Where are you going?' He answered me, 'To measure Jerusalem, to see what is its width and what is its length.' Then the angel who talked with me came forward, and another angel came forward to meet him, and said to him, 'Run, say to that young man: Jerusalem shall be inhabited like villages without walls, because of the multitude of people and animals in it. For I will be a wall of fire all round it, says the Lord, and I will be the glory within it.'

I love Mothering Sunday not just for its celebration of my being in a family, but for its reminder of how my Christian allegiance makes me part of God's never-ending family the church. In the Prayer Book service, there is a Jerusalem mention today through the use of Galatians 4:26 affirming that Jerusalem is 'above', 'free' and 'our mother'. In past ages, people made return visits today to 'mother' parish churches from daughter churches and the day remains a pointer to our ultimate 'mother church' that exists in heaven.

Like the later writings of Isaiah, Zechariah writes of the joyous restoration of Jerusalem after the people's return there from exile in Babylon in 538BC at the edict of King Cyrus of Persia. In this passage, Zechariah is interrogating a man with a measuring line set to do what this Bible study series is geared to do in a wider sense: namely, to measure Jerusalem, to see what is its width and what is its length. To do so is to take stock of our experience of exile from God, his repeated offers of restoration and the joy of those who take him at his word. Such joy is implied in Zechariah's picture of Jerusalem inhabited like villages without walls, because of the multitude of people and animals in it. God promises to be a wall of fire all round and to be the glory within the city. There is no more joyous place than a heart purified by the fire of the Holy Spirit!

Lord, we thank you today for your purifying Spirit
and for membership of your holy church.

JOHN TWISLETON

Pray for the peace of Jerusalem

I was glad when they said to me, 'Let us go to the house of the Lord!' Our feet are standing within your gates, O Jerusalem. Jerusalem – built as a city that is bound firmly together. To it the tribes go up, the tribes of the Lord… Pray for the peace of Jerusalem: 'May they prosper who love you. Peace be within your walls, and security within your towers.'

How much I find myself praying for peace in the world! As I look through the Bible, what I read about Jerusalem is both an encouragement and challenge to that prayer. Jerusalem first gets on the map when King David gathered the tribes of the Lord after capturing the old Jebusite fortress, which stood in geographic 'neutrality' between the northern and southern tribes. It became 'the city of David' (2 Samuel 5:9), a seat of central government as tribal elders ceded authority to the king. The tribes' allegiance was further cemented by David's rescue from oblivion of the ark of the covenant, sign of God's presence with his people, and bringing it in state to Jerusalem. David believed God made a special covenant with Israel through anointing him so any king who was descended from him would receive God's favour.

Psalm 122 is linked to David as a pilgrimage 'song of Zion', written for worship in the temple (built by David's son, Solomon) for the ark. It is a reminder of Jerusalem's association with worship, taken up in the book of Revelation as well as many Christian hymns.

In this psalm, a major focus is unity: 'O Jerusalem… built as a city that is bound firmly together… Pray for the peace of Jerusalem… Peace be within your walls, and security within your towers.'

My prayer for the peace of Jerusalem flows from God's heart for the world and for his church. Even with many denominations in the church today, still we rejoice at our worldwide Christian citizenship of mystic 'Jerusalem'.

Lord Jesus, make your church more effective in its task of gathering the nations into the peace of God's kingdom.

JOHN TWISLETON

Think only on Jerusalem

Although Daniel knew that the document [forbidding prayer] had been signed, he continued to go to his house, which had windows in its upper room open towards Jerusalem, and to get down on his knees three times a day to pray to his God and praise him, just as he had done previously. The conspirators came and found Daniel praying and seeking mercy before his God. Then they approached the king and... the king gave the command, and Daniel was brought and thrown into the den of lions... God sent his angel and shut the lions' mouths.

I love Westminster Abbey evensong, beautifully sung day by day, interspersed with delightfully human moments such as the chaos caused when the large and very mixed congregation turns to face east during the Creed. This action of turning east to say the Christian Creed in the UK, originating from this passage in the book of Daniel, honours the givenness of our faith in Jesus Christ, born of the Virgin Mary, suffered under Pontius Pilate, crucified, died and rose again. These events provide a strong base for our faith, which stands or falls not on our perceptions of God, but on God's revelation of himself in history, witnessed to by the Bible.

The book of Daniel contains stories of how God's people fared in their 6th-century BC exile in Babylon. In this passage, we read how God stood by Daniel and answered his prayers offered in the face of vicious persecution under the Persian King Darius. Daniel's longing for Jerusalem features in the structuring of his prayer facing the holy city. This practice of prayer, facing Jerusalem, continues today in churches that use the Book of Common Prayer. We turn in heart and mind, like Daniel, to Jerusalem, seeking a strengthening of faith through our worship.

Jerusalem as a place is made holy by the ultimate revelation of God in Jesus Christ, who died in our place, as sinners, to live in our place as those renewed by his Spirit.

Lord, with Daniel we turn to you today in fellowship with so many persecuted Christians. As we look to you, keep us steadfast in allegiance to you, for Jesus' sake.

JOHN TWISLETON

Building Jerusalem

Many nations shall come and say: 'Come, let us go up to the mountain of the Lord, to the house of the God of Jacob; that he may teach us his ways and that we may walk in his paths.' For out of Zion shall go forth instruction, and the word of the Lord from Jerusalem.

In this dynamic, international vision, the prophet Micah presents Jerusalem as the religious centre of the world. Found there is a two-fold spiritual movement of nations to God and the carrying forth of divine instruction. The passage invites us to ponder how we balance the call of God and our response. It is by his invitation that we stand consciously in his presence and serve him today.

William Blake's 'Jerusalem', set to memorable music by Hubert Parry, is increasingly England's national song. Its enigmatic nature, linked to the Glastonbury myth of Christ's visiting here, does not subtract from the solid aspiration it conveys of building Jerusalem on England's shores. Jerusalem is God's city, and we pray that our own cities and towns may be God's too, as we work for the kingdom of this world to become the kingdom of our Lord and of his Messiah (see Revelation 11:15b).

Jerusalem retains to this day the dynamic Micah describes, in both its physical and mystical reality. In his book, *Jerusalem: The biography*, Simon Sebag Montefiore describes the city as a two-way mirror revealing her inner life while reflecting the world outside. Whether it was the epoch of total faith, righteous empire building, evangelical revelation or secular nationalism, Jerusalem became its symbol and its prize. But like the mirrors in a circus, the reflections can be distorted.

I remember vividly my own visit to Jerusalem, as part of an international pilgrimage, bringing into my spirit this very ambivalence. I found myself weeping where Jesus wept at his sacrifice there for me and for all, and seeing tears released also at the evidence of sinful division there and in the rest of the world, so out of sync with that love.

O God, open our hearts this day to know more fully our need of your mercy, shown to us in our Saviour Jesus Christ.

JOHN TWISLETON

Vindication of faith

For Zion's sake I will not keep silent, and for Jerusalem's sake I will not rest, until her vindication shines out like the dawn, and her salvation like a burning torch. The nations shall see your vindication, and all the kings your glory; and you shall be called by a new name that the mouth of the Lord will give. You shall be a crown of beauty in the hand of the Lord, and a royal diadem in the hand of your God.

Because Jerusalem is both terrestrial and celestial, she exists in several dimensions. The choice of the feminine pronoun for the city in Isaiah links to her perceived beauty. This is taken up in the Christian revelation of God and his church – those who are participants in the divine nature (2 Peter 1:4). Through repentance, faith and baptism, we are made children of God and, so made, reflect our parentage.

When Isaiah speaks of Jerusalem's vindication, demonstrated after the Jewish exile, he anticipates how accepting Christ's sacrifice for their sins will remake and beautify Christian believers: 'You shall be a crown of beauty in the hand of the Lord, and a royal diadem in the hand of your God' (v. 3). If Jerusalem, with all its tribulations and shortcomings, is beautiful in God's eyes, how much more are believers? Their vindication will shine forth in eternity.

Austin Farrer, picking up on these words of Isaiah, writes of the saints being ultimately like a heavenly corona over the shining beauty of the Trinity. The diadem, like Jerusalem itself, can be seen as a coming together of people, of the redeemed having the power to comprehend, with all the saints, what is the breadth and length and height and depth, and to know the love of Christ that surpasses knowledge (Ephesians 3:18–19a).

The vision of heaven in the Bible is nothing individualistic. Though scripture makes plain God's gift to us of his Son is for individuals to welcome, its every vision of the world to come is, like Jerusalem, a city with responsible citizenship who enjoy God together, with all the saints.

Lord, may we become more fully what we are made to be,
resplendent in your beauty.

JOHN TWISLETON

Jerusalem's lament

From daughter Zion has departed all her majesty. Her princes have become like stags that find no pasture; they fled without strength before the pursuer. Jerusalem remembers, in the days of her affliction and wandering, all the precious things that were hers in days of old. When her people fell into the hand of the foe, and there was no one to help her, the foe looked on mocking over her downfall. Jerusalem sinned grievously, so she has become a mockery; all who honoured her despise her, for they have seen her nakedness; she herself groans, and turns her face away.

I can never forget going to a church in Holy Week to hear the haunting service of Tenebrae. The word is Latin for 'darkness', and this service involves extinguishing candles one by one while listening to a sung version of the book of Lamentations. In the original Hebrew, this passage has verses beginning with words that form an alphabet – from Aleph to Taw. Each letter is sung at the start of each verse in a haunting chant, with the chorus calling for Jerusalem to turn back to God.

We can imagine a remnant gathering singing this lament around the temple ruins during the Jewish exile in 597 to 540BC. It acknowledges judgement from God, while calling for vindication and the defeat of the occupying foe. Jerusalem, the sinful, needy and exiled community, is seen in Christianity as a pointer to the universal sinfulness and need of mercy addressed by God in Jesus Christ.

Lent is a good time to refresh our examination of conscience to recapture our individual need of that divine mercy. Many prepare a sacramental confession to voice their sins aloud before Easter. This voicing has power to bind sin and is coupled to the grace of individual welcome home to God pronounced by the priest.

In her sin and restoration, Jerusalem symbolises the fragility and beauty of human beings. In building up the historical city, and allowing her flight from the Lord to precede confession of sin and restoration, God is modelling in his word a pattern of church life for us in the 21st century.

Lord Jesus Christ, Son of God, have mercy on me, a sinner.

JOHN TWISLETON

Holy impatience

This city has aroused my anger and wrath, from the day it was built until this day, so that I will remove it from my sight because of all the evil of the people of Israel and the people of Judah that they did to provoke me to anger – they, their kings and their officials, their priests and their prophets, the citizens of Judah and the inhabitants of Jerusalem. They have turned their backs to me, not their faces; though I have taught them persistently, they would not listen and accept correction.

It is not that long since the Church of the Holy Sepulchre in Jerusalem completed a much-delayed restoration. This passage on God's anger against Jerusalem came to mind as I looked back on my own visit to the church, when I was greatly saddened to observe evidence of disunity within this city that Psalm 122:3 describes as being 'bound firmly together'.

Impatience and anger are linked. When God sees wrongs to be righted he is impatient, even if one day is 1,000 years to him, and angry. Such righteous anger contrasts with the human anger one sees flaring up at times, in and, of course, away from Jerusalem. In creating the world and human free will, God opened the world up to such retrograde action that he would need to counter.

Yet Jerusalem is key witness to the redeeming love that stretched out its arms outside her walls. On my pilgrimage I had the privilege of offering the Eucharist near the site of Christ's crucifixion. It was brought home to me how that obedient action of self-offering has potential, wherever it is celebrated, to build unity. Christ's offering for sin in Jerusalem has power to free and save the world, which makes the Eucharist the cleansing and healing rite it is.

Is there any impatience within you today?
Is it godly impatience or otherwise?

JOHN TWISLETON

Citizens of Zion

Thus says the Lord: I will return to Zion, and will dwell in the midst of Jerusalem; Jerusalem shall be called the faithful city, and the mountain of the Lord of hosts shall be called the holy mountain. Thus says the Lord of hosts: Old men and old women shall again sit in the streets of Jerusalem, each with staff in hand because of their great age. And the streets of the city shall be full of boys and girls playing in its streets. Thus says the Lord of hosts: Even though it seems impossible to the remnant of this people in these days, should it also seem impossible to me, says the Lord of hosts?

Zechariah anticipated, with other post-exile prophets, the return of those exiled from Jerusalem to live in security with the blessing of long life. God says 'I will return to Zion' (the mount of Jerusalem) and quizzes those who doubt this restoration, asking 'Should it... seem impossible to me?' When God promises something, he delivers. We must keep faith in his promises, which we now know to be fulfilled in yet another dimension.

On this first Sunday in Passiontide, Lent changes gear as the cross comes to the centre of the liturgy alongside Christ's promise: 'I, when I am lifted up from the earth, will draw all people to myself' (John 12:32). Through his Son's death and resurrection, Zechariah's prophecy that God will return and dwell among his people by his Spirit finds more profound fulfilment. The church can be seen as Holy Zion, Christ and Christians inseparable – God and humanity reconciled. Paradoxically, this mystical Jerusalem was first created outside the walls of the terrestrial city on Mount Calvary. There we see restoration of the people of God through the establishing of the forgiveness of sins, the resurrection of the body and the life everlasting (the Apostles' Creed).

Today, on this Sunday of the Passion, mindful of that amazing grace, we citizens of new Jerusalem pray: 'Saviour, since of Zion's city, I through grace a member am. Let the world deride or pity, I will glory in thy name' (John Newton, 1725–1807).

JOHN TWISLETON

Come to my Father's house

Now every year his parents went to Jerusalem for the festival of the Passover. And when he was twelve years old, they went up as usual for the festival. When the festival was ended and they started to return, the boy Jesus stayed behind in Jerusalem, but his parents did not know it... After three days they found him in the temple, sitting among the teachers, listening to them and asking them questions. And all who heard him were amazed at his understanding and his answers... He said to them, 'Why were you searching for me? Did you not know that I must be in my Father's house?'

The coming of Mary's son to the temple brightens Jerusalem. In this story of Mary and Joseph's temple visit with the boy Jesus, we see him sitting among the teachers, listening to them and asking them questions. Here wisdom is revealed at many levels: he is God made flesh, and serves as an example to us of attentiveness to scripture and its interpreters within the household of faith. Firstly, the story evidences how Jesus was extraordinary from the start of his earthly life. Secondly, though we don't have to go to temple or, rather, church nowadays to be informed about the Bible, the passage has a warning. Only by listening to and asking questions of our own priests and fellow church members can we see our Bible knowledge distilled into wisdom for living. There is great value in the discipline of spiritual direction or companionship in attaining such wisdom.

'Did you not know that I must be in my Father's house?' Jesus says to his parents and, through this scripture, asks us the same questions: did you not know that the sacrifices offered here are for me to fulfil here in Jerusalem? Did you not know that the temple I am to serve in my indestructible priesthood (Hebrews 7:16) is in the New Jerusalem, which is to be yours?

Lord Jesus, I seek to be with you for ever in your Father's house.

JOHN TWISLETON

New Jerusalem's foundation

Then the devil took [Jesus] to the holy city and placed him on the pinnacle of the temple, saying to him, 'If you are the Son of God, throw yourself down; for it is written, "He will command his angels concerning you", and "On their hands they will bear you up, so that you will not dash your foot against a stone."' Jesus said to him, 'Again it is written, "Do not put the Lord your God to the test."'

'I'm the king of the castle – you're the dirty rascal,' children used to sing in vying for the highest place, and behind that chant is an age-old truth. To gain higher ground is a military advantage. In the world of the Bible, high ground symbolises ascendant power, which is why mountains often come into play. The temple had prominence over the heights of Jerusalem itself, sited on Mount Zion, towering above the valley of Kidron. So far as the temple pinnacle goes, we're hard pressed to place it since the last temple was destroyed by the Romans in 70AD after the Jewish rebellion.

In the account of the Lord's temptation, we go beyond the surface of things into the spiritual conflict of divine redemption. Like the next temptation he offers, which sees Jesus taken up a high mountain, the devil seeks to show him a way of physical triumph and wonder working. The lust for power that so bedevils the earthly Jerusalem to this day is categorically rejected as having any relevance in the new Jerusalem.

In this liturgical season of Passiontide, we read Paul's summary of the redemption effected in Jerusalem by Jesus Christ who, 'though he was in the form of God, did not regard equality with God as something to be exploited, but emptied himself… and became obedient to the point of death – even death on a cross. Therefore God also highly exalted him and gave him the name that is above every name' (Philippians 2:6–7a, 8b–9).

O God, rebuild our lives on the solid base of humility and love
shown in your Son, our Saviour Jesus Christ.

JOHN TWISLETON

The gift of the Eucharist

[Jesus] took a loaf of bread, and when he had given thanks, he broke it and gave it to them, saying, 'This is my body, which is given for you. Do this in remembrance of me.' And he did the same with the cup after supper, saying, 'This cup that is poured out for you is the new covenant in my blood.'

I go back to Jerusalem daily. I do so by going to the cenacle (or upper room), place of the last supper, through the Eucharist. This saying of Jesus in Luke 22, replicated in 1 Corinthians 11:25, has had more conse-quence than most verses in the Bible, for has ever a command been so much obeyed?

The statements 'This is my body... my blood' were first made over bread and wine before the Lord's death, making plain his intention on Calvary. The obedient repetition of that action he calls for is at the heart of church order. Little later than the canon of scripture was finalised at the end of the second century saw the emergence of bishops, priests and deacons to teach and to lead this action after the death of the apostles.

The narrative of the institution of the Eucharist continues in Paul's ver-sion: 'For as often as you eat this bread and drink the cup, you proclaim the Lord's death until he comes' (1 Corinthians 11:25). To proclaim or, lit-erally, 'show' the Lord's death is our main Christian education and forma-tion. The once-for-all saving action in Jerusalem is carried into every place and age by the Holy Spirit and apostolic order, the action of self-giving, death, resurrection and the coming of the Holy Spirit.

As we take, bless, break and share bread and wine, we show Christ's death before God for the good of the world and get drawn into a fuller death to sin and anointing in the Holy Spirit.

Lord Jesus Christ, in a wonderful sacrament you have left to us
a memorial of your suffering, death and resurrection in Jerusalem.
May our devout participation in Holy Communion allow that
saving action to bear fruit in our lives.

JOHN TWISLETON

Jerusalem, our joy

When the day of Pentecost had come, they were all together in one place. And suddenly from heaven there came a sound like the rush of a violent wind, and it filled the entire house where they were sitting. Divided tongues, as of fire, appeared among them, and a tongue rested on each of them. All of them were filled with the Holy Spirit and began to speak in other languages, as the Spirit gave them ability... The word of God continued to spread; the number of the disciples increased greatly in Jerusalem.

The buoyant joy of that Pentecost feast and the acts of the apostles following Christ's death and resurrection are linked to access to God offered to all by the Holy Spirit, starting at Jerusalem. One of the most famous religious songs, 'The Holy City' by Michael Maybrick (1841–1913), captures this scene just weeks after the shadow of a cross arose upon a lonely hill, in which the resurrection and the gift of the Spirit give the first believers anticipation of access to the Holy City in its splendour to come:

'And once again the scene was changed, new earth there seemed to be. I saw the Holy City beside the timeless sea. The light of God was on its streets, the gates were open wide, and all who would might enter, and no one was denied... Jerusalem! Jerusalem! Sing for the night is o'er! Hosanna in the highest! Hosanna forevermore!'

This song captures the joy of heaven that spilled out 20 centuries ago on to the streets of Jerusalem, which is ours to recover today. As the Acts of the Apostles also remind us, joy in the risen Lord Jesus is a sustainer through tribulation and persecution, which have so often preceded astonishing church growth, as reported in Acts 6:7.

Lord Jesus, we open our hearts to your Holy Spirit to welcome your presence. As we turn to you in penitence and faith this day, come to us and grant us a fresh anointing in joy, so others can also be touched by you through us. By your grace may the prayers and acts of your followers serve to complete the work you began in Jerusalem.

JOHN TWISLETON

The church will triumph

In the spirit [one of the seven angels] carried me away to a great, high mountain and showed me the holy city Jerusalem coming down out of heaven from God. It has the glory of God and a radiance like a very rare jewel, like jasper, clear as crystal. It has a great, high wall with twelve gates, and at the gates twelve angels, and on the gates are inscribed the names of the twelve tribes of the Israelites; on the east three gates, on the north three gates, on the south three gates, and on the west three gates. And the wall of the city has twelve foundations, and on them are the twelve names of the twelve apostles of the Lamb.

I love the description we have here of the new Jerusalem, which comes from the book of Revelation to John. He has earlier (Revelation 17:3, 5) been carried into the wilderness to view the whore (Babylon). Now, by contrast, we are caught up with him on high to view the spouse (Jerusalem). This is God's spouse, the bride of Christ the heavenly bridegroom, God's church filled by his Spirit to radiate like a very rare jewel, like jasper, clear as crystal. It is awesome to think of the church's glory made equal to God's. It is however a consolation, in the face of the sin prevalent in the world today, to know that the church's divinity will ultimately prevail in the purposes of God.

In John's vision of the Jerusalem who is 'above', 'free' and 'our mother' (Galatians 4:26), we see once again the significance of building on the faith and witness of the apostles who were entrusted with Christ's mandate for the church on Easter Sunday: 'As the Father has sent me, so I send you… Receive the Holy Spirit' (John 20:21–22). Twelve gates, tribes and apostles affirm continuity between old covenant and new covenant, reaching forward into the apostolic order and vitality of the church in our age.

O God, thank you for the triumphant vision you give us through John. When the going gets tough, keep our eyes on Jesus and the Jerusalem above.

JOHN TWISLETON

Jerusalem, our hope and joy

You have come to Mount Zion and to the city of the living God, the heavenly Jerusalem, and to innumerable angels in festal gathering, and to the assembly of the firstborn who are enrolled in heaven, and to God the judge of all, and to the spirits of the righteous made perfect, and to Jesus, the mediator of a new covenant, and to the sprinkled blood that speaks a better word than the blood of Abel. See that you do not refuse the one who is speaking.

I find the letter to the Hebrews one of the most eye-opening sections of the Bible. It comes from one whose Christian vision is well forged, to Jewish Christian believers suffering intense persecution. The writer points to the risen Lord as eternal priest and victim, fulfiller of the old covenant and in his sameness yesterday, today and for ever the brilliant cause of hope and joy (Hebrews 13:8).

In these verses, past, present and future come together in Jesus Christ. We come here and now to him in worship through his sprinkled blood that both looks back to Sinai and forward to the new Jerusalem. On Mount Sinai, thunder and smoke indicated the separation of God's world and ours in the old covenant, which has now melted into union. Christians approach the altar of God with angels and archangels and all the company of heaven, and are not below these celestial beings. Such it is to come to Mount Zion and to the city of the living God, the heavenly Jerusalem.

As we look forward to Sunday worship at the start of Holy Week, this passage from Hebrews has special resonance as we set our hearts afresh upon Jesus Christ in Jerusalem then, now and for eternity. Let us not refuse the one who is speaking as we continue to ponder the scriptures and discover their meaning and power.

Truly Jerusalem name we that shore, vision of peace that brings joy evermore; wish and fulfilment can severed be ne'er, nor the thing hoped for come short of the prayer (Peter Abelard, 1079–1142 and John Neale, 1818–66).

JOHN TWISLETON

Holy Week

Poems and songs have an amazing capacity to get deep into us. Their words and their pauses, their melodies and their rhythms can become part of us. The feelings they produce can shape us, a soundtrack for the day, a liturgy even for our lives.

This Holy Week, in an attempt to enter and to glimpse the events of Holy Week from Jesus' perspective, we'll spend time with some of the poem-songs that might have shaped him in the week leading up to his death. On Palm Sunday, we'll hear the chants of the people as Jesus entered Jerusalem. These songs of honour and welcome must have had an impact upon him. They would surely have been welcome. But, confronted with the fickle nature of the people's praise, Jesus would soon have had to go elsewhere for the deep resources he required to face the brutal rejection that came his way.

This Holy Week, we will engage with the psalms set for the principal service each day. We can be reasonably confident that Jesus would have known many, if not all, of the psalms by heart. The psalms formed the great word and song book of the Jewish faith in which he was steeped. The Gospel writers Mark and Matthew reported that a line from the psalms was on the lips of Jesus during the crucifixion, and we can imagine that he dug deep into his memory of the psalms to navigate the cruel demands of his betrayal, trial, abandonment and crucifixion.

I have a particularly powerful personal memory of a group reading of Psalm 88 in a cell beneath the Church of St Peter in Gallicantu in Jerusalem, a possible site for Jesus' imprisonment following his arrest in Gethsemane. 'I am counted among those who go down to the Pit', we read. 'I am like those who have no help, like those forsaken among the dead.' In that moment, it felt as if we were there with Jesus – and as if the abandonment of Jesus was meeting all our own experiences of abandonment.

Whatever you face this Holy Week, may the songs of this season create space for any experience of descent. May they also, in God's grace, sustain you in faith, in hope and in love.

IAN ADAMS

Our sense of worth

Many people spread their cloaks on the road, and others spread leafy branches that they had cut in the fields. Then those who went ahead and those who followed were shouting, "Hosanna! Blessed is the one who comes in the name of the Lord! Blessed is the coming kingdom of our ancestor David! Hosanna in the highest heaven!" Then he entered Jerusalem and went into the temple; and when he had looked around at everything, as it was already late, he went out to Bethany with the twelve.

It's great to be recognised. It's lovely to be praised. And it's wonderful whenever our work is honoured. But we cannot let our well-being rest on us being recognised, praised or honoured. As lovely as such songs will be to our ear, they are all passing. Our sense of worth has to rest elsewhere. Jesus soon discovered (if he didn't already know) that public acclamation is a fleeting and capricious thing. Of course, the praises of the crowd must have been welcome when they came. Such apparent recognition of the greater story to which Jesus was giving himself – of God's kingdom coming close – must have been pleasing. He had, after all, plenty of experience already of scorn and rejection. But things were about to change.

In today's reading Mark's remark that 'it was already late' subtly hints that the time of praise and recognition for Jesus had already gone. The crowds had melted away, and that evening, alone with the twelve, he left the city that had given him such a glorious welcome only hours before. A few palm leaves discarded in the street, and occasional voices breaking the night's silence, were perhaps the only reminders of the praises that had been made, the songs that had been sung.

While being thankful for any recognition, praise or honour that may have come *our* way, can we set any such encouragements aside, and recognise that our sense of belonging can and must lie elsewhere? In tomorrow's reading and reflection we will reflect on the nature of that *elsewhere*.

On who or what does your sense of well-being rest at this time?

IAN ADAMS

A true pivot point

How precious is your steadfast love, O God! All people may take refuge in the shadow of your wings. They feast on the abundance of your house, and you give them drink from the river of your delights. For with you is the fountain of life; in your light we see light.

The praises of the crowds may have been welcome, but Jesus surely knew that his sense of worth and well-being had to rest on something stronger than such fleeting moments. We can imagine Jesus going to a psalm such as this one to seek out a true and lasting pivot point on which to balance his sense of being.

The 'steadfast love of God' was the psalmist's comfort, and so it had become the source of the strength of Jesus. And it's instructive to see how the psalm depicts this divine love in engagement with the demands of human existence. Whenever we find ourselves under pressure, the temptation is to fold in on ourselves. We can find ourselves imagining limits to goodness, or constructing boundaries to fence off the provision of God from ourselves or others. We may begin to see around us only scarcity, and we lose our sense of abundance.

But the psalmist, rooted in the steadfast love of God, sees no limits to goodness, constructs no boundaries to God's provision and only sees abundance. Stumbling over him/herself in a torrent of metaphors, the psalmist proclaims that God's steadfast love is a refuge, a feast, a river of delights, a fountain of life, and a light in which we may see light! What an astonishing collection – all leaning towards one great insight, that the means to live a deeply fruitful human life is discoverable and is found through being rooted in the love of God.

Amidst the experiences of scarcity and darkness faced by Jesus that Holy Week, we can imagine this psalm renewing his sense that neither scarcity nor darkness would have the last word. Other words would be uttered: words of recognition, words of peace, words of love.

Reflect on your current experience of scarcity and abundance.
What, if anything, in those experiences is true?

IAN ADAMS

Retribution – or compassion?

O God, do not be far from me; O my God, make haste to help me! Let my accusers be put to shame and consumed; let those who seek to hurt me be covered with scorn and disgrace. But I will hope continually, and will praise you yet more and more.

In today's reading, the psalmist gets personal. Threats from some exterior or unknown source may be one thing, and tough enough to face. Personal betrayals and accusations can feel like something else. Our desire for recompense or for retribution can take on great power, threatening to consume the one who has been accused or betrayed as much as the accuser or betrayer. How soon a cycle of destruction picks up speed. How hard to slow it down.

We know that, in Holy Week, Jesus had to face such realities. And we know too that there were times when, as a result, he felt himself to be alone. In the garden. In the cell. On the cross. The darkness before him threatened to become too hard to bear. 'O God, do not be far from me; O my God, make haste to help me!' And finally, a deep sense of abandonment.

How did he survive this? It seems that Jesus chose not to ignore or belittle the toughness of what he was going through. He gave both space and voice to the darkness, to the descent, to the despair that he was encountering. The reality of whatever is happening cannot and must not be ignored.

But, inspired perhaps in part by psalms such as this one, Jesus managed to keep to the course that seemed to be calling him. Amazingly, he appears not to have struck out in thought, word or action against his accusers. In this, he seems to have parted company with the (understandable) desire of the psalmist to see the purveyors of injustice get their due reward. Jesus' sense of being rooted in God's love – and in his love for God – seems to have enabled him to nurture a deep compassion for those who had betrayed or accused him.

What is causing you hurt you at this time? What might a prayer of hope sound like in this context?

IAN ADAMS

You are my help and my deliverer

Be pleased, O God, to deliver me. O Lord, make haste to help me… Let all who seek you rejoice and be glad in you… But I am poor and needy; hasten to me, O God! You are my help and my deliverer; O Lord, do not delay!

The psalms are such a gift. Whatever we are going through, their poems and songs go with us. They understand how we are feeling, refusing to offer any easy (and false) solution to our troubles, whilst holding on to the possibility of hope rooted in the love of God. And, in this Holy Week, they provide a soundscape to an ever-deepening sense of claustrophobia. The walls are closing in on Jesus. Options are running out. We can imagine him praying 'Be pleased, O God, to deliver me. O Lord, make haste to help me!' And we can hear the silence that follows.

It may be tempting to move on to a psalm that is more overt in its sense of hope, but that is not helpful. The gift of the psalms is to be found in our agreeing for them to do their gradual work upon us. So how are we to work with psalms like this? Classically, in both the Jewish faith and in Christian monastic life, repetition of the psalms is seen to be vital. Perhaps our experience of working with the psalms this Holy Week may inspire us to make them a more regular part of our daily prayer and worship, or confirm us in that practice.

Another tradition is to take a line from the psalm and allow that to become our prayer. Through gradual repetition of this phrase, we may find that the gift of the psalm gradually opens up within us. In taking into ourselves a line like 'You are my help and my deliverer', we may discover the reality that this line suggests. The deliverance may not come in the way we had imagined it, but the tradition of the psalms, and the tradition of Jesus, promise that deliverance will nevertheless, in God's grace, in God's way, come.

What line or phrase from today's psalm, if any,
seems to resonate with you?

IAN ADAMS

A crucial question

I walk before the Lord in the land of the living. I kept my faith, even when I said, 'I am greatly afflicted'; I said in my consternation, 'Everyone is a liar.' What shall I return to the Lord for all his bounty to me? I will lift up the cup of salvation and call on the name of the Lord, I will pay my vows to the Lord in the presence of all his people.

'What shall I return to the Lord, for all his bounty to me?' This question was a crucial one for the psalmist; as it was in turn for Jesus in Holy Week; and now perhaps for us too. It's a question that asks what is motivating us, seeking to understand what it might be that will help us to persist when all is falling apart, even when we are 'greatly afflicted', and when 'everyone is a liar'. It's about our calling, our reason for being.

The psalmist's answer – 'I will lift up the cup of salvation' – was a further evolution of the question, and amounted to a rededication to his/her craft. Jesus' answer was what enabled him to walk the sorrowful way to the cross. And for all of us who seek now to follow in the footsteps of the Christ, the question is – how might *we* lift up the cup of salvation?

The answer is not a one size and shape fits all. Your lifting up the cup of salvation, your returning to the Lord – while being similar in spirit to that of the psalmist – will be unique to you. The answer will be shaped by your story, your experience, your setting and your calling.

When we can articulate a sense of what our calling is, we have in God's grace a wonderful means to navigate this Holy Week – and all the demanding weeks that will come our way in the future. Our answer will be a guiding light to which we will keep on returning.

What do you sense is your calling at this time?
What are you being called to return to the Lord,
and how are you being called to lift up the cup of salvation?

IAN ADAMS

All is lost

My God, my God, why have you forsaken me? Why are you so far from helping me, from the words of my groaning? O my God, I cry by day, but you do not answer; and by night, but find no rest. Yet you are holy, enthroned on the praises of Israel. In you our ancestors trusted; they trusted, and you delivered them. To you they cried, and were saved; in you they trusted, and were not put to shame… Do not be far from me, for trouble is near and there is no one to help.

Today we reach the darkest moment yet of this Holy Week. Jesus is crucified, and all appears to be lost. And Psalm 22 as a soundtrack to the day is perfect in its bleakness. No wonder that, in his agony on the cross, Jesus reached for this psalm. 'My God, my God, why have you forsaken me?' No easy words of comfort here. 'Why are you so far from helping me, from the words of my groaning?' Brutal reality. The only comfort for the psalmist appears to be some slim hope in the holiness of God, and a distant memory of God's faithfulness to ancestors.

It's so important that we enter into the wild despair of Good Friday and the blank loss of Holy Saturday. These days cannot be glossed over. For this is how life can be – and how it is this very day for so many around the world and down your street, where 'trouble is near and there is no one to help'. Only through facing and acknowledging the reality of life's toughness may we authentically experience, offer and speak of any hope to come.

This dive into the depths of Good Friday and Holy Saturday is a challenge. Not to imagine Sunday coming can feel like a dangerous thing. But only by taking this adventurous path may we truly be open to experiencing the wonder of whatever may follow…

How might you enter into the loss of Good Friday? Who can you be alongside today in their experience of forsakenness?

IAN ADAMS

Grief and glory

I have never been able to figure out why most of us find it easier to observe Lent than Easter. Churches run Lent groups, not Easter ones. You would think we might be glad of a chance to focus on the uplifting aspects of our faith, rather than those about our failings and the need for repentance; but, no, we spend six weeks thinking about how much we need Jesus' sacrifice on the cross and similar themes – much-needed, but actually rather grim. And after Easter Day dawns, we struggle to get our heads round the weeks of rejoicing.

Often, of course, the world offers us little to celebrate, in all its horrors and the cruelties we inflict on each other, which are so much part of our fallen existence. And yet we know that is not the full picture. Christ is risen. He has overcome death. So the mysterious tension between this triumph and the griefs of every day is something that we have to work out, every day. Sometimes one will seem to dominate; sometimes the other. But it is all within the overarching knowledge that God has won already; good has beaten evil. God's love has changed everything.

I am writing these eight days of notes about Easter from a particular place regarding the business of death, because my doctors have told me that I am not likely to live more than a year. Cancer has spread through my body, and I will die sooner rather than later: in a superficial sense, death will have beaten me. But… I still know that this is not the full picture. God will not be destroyed by death. He will still be there to hold me up, and to continue his constant love towards me and those around me.

In these reflections, I would like to explore a little of this tension between, on the one hand, the pain and limits of earthly existence, and on the other, the eternal hope we have in God – the God whose love for each one of us is not ended by our physical death.

RACHEL BOULDING

Hauled out of the darkness

Now there was a garden in the place where he was crucified, and in the garden there was a new tomb in which no one had ever been laid. And so, because it was the Jewish day of Preparation, and the tomb was nearby, they laid Jesus there.

This must be the strangest day in the Christian year – a day when nothing is meant to happen. There are not usually any church services during the daytime, while the events that are being marked are the waiting of the disciples and the laying of Jesus in the tomb. Church tradition also designates this time as that of the Harrowing of Hell, which is referred to in the Apostles' Creed (the short one, that is usually said at Evening Prayer): 'He descended into hell.' The scene is often depicted in paintings and in the icons of the Eastern Orthodox Church, in which Jesus is seen hauling Adam and Eve out of their infernal prison – often grabbing them firmly and dragging them out fairly roughly.

This can be a strangely reassuring image. Jesus is coming to fetch people, using all his might, and heave them into the light. He is rescuing humankind, taking the initiative to save us. Whatever mess we have got ourselves into, he is here to lift us out. This is rather like the rest of our life: God loves us into existence, giving us talents and opportunities (as he did with the people of Israel throughout the Old Testament), but we muck things up, squandering his wondrous gifts and creation. Yet God gives us more chances, in the end sending his Son and dragging us up towards his marvellous love, if we will let him.

So, in this day of expectant waiting, we might spare a few moments to ponder our need for God's help. It becomes a bit like Advent, as we pause in the darkness of our fears and hopes, and look forward to God's coming. Despite our frazzled preparations – Easter gardens, triumphant music, flowers, lamb dinners and all those chocolate eggs – the purpose matters most. This is the calm moment, before the boisterous joy of the night vigil and tomorrow's celebrations.

Father, save me from my selfish darkness, and drag me into your marvellous light.

RACHEL BOULDING

He has been raised

As they entered the tomb, they saw a young man, dressed in a white robe, sitting on the right side; and they were alarmed. But he said to them, 'Do not be alarmed; you are looking for Jesus of Nazareth, who was crucified. He has been raised; he is not here. Look, there is the place they laid him. But go, tell his disciples and Peter that he is going ahead of you to Galilee; there you will see him, just as he told you.'

After the strangest day comes the most amazing one – although it is still wrapped in mystery. Extremes of grief, abandonment, and utter hopelessness are transformed. No wonder we struggle to take it in. We are bewildered and overwhelmed. As we saw yesterday, God has been infinitely patient and unfailingly loving to us, despite our petty rebellions and cherished selfishness. And now he gives yet again. He never abandons us, and is always reaching out to us.

We can celebrate without any shadows of trouble. God has done this great deed, conquering death. It is a time of pure joy. I hope you have the chance to celebrate in a suitably delightful way. Some churches manage to do this with bells, klaxons and fire at the Easter Vigil service the night before. Then, the deepest darkness that can be mustered is pushed back, candle by single candle, going from pew to pew, lit from a great bonfire. The light of Christ drives out the lingering gloom.

And yet, even here, Jesus bears the scars of suffering. The young man in white calls him 'Jesus of Nazareth, who was crucified': he is a man from a particular place, who was killed. But he is fully God, too, and he has been raised from the darkness of the grave. So every one of us, who are each marked by the particular scars from both what we have done to ourselves and what others have done to us, are brought to new life with him.

Father God, in your love, you have given us your Son, and raised him from death. Work in me to bring your infinite life and joy into all the deadly places of my existence.

RACHEL BOULDING

Fear amid the rejoicing

But he said to them, 'Do not be alarmed… But go, tell his disciples and Peter that he is going ahead of you to Galilee; there you will see him, just as he told you.' So they went out and fled from the tomb, for terror and amazement had seized them; and they said nothing to anyone, for they were afraid.

After the world was turned upside down yesterday, we may be rejoicing, but we are still overwhelmed by a maelstrom of alarm, terror and amazement. We are celebrating, but we cannot altogether cast off the grieving of the past few days. Jesus' resurrection has not come out of nowhere: it has emerged from betrayal, torture and the deepest psychological, emotional and physical pain. Our past suffering lingers about us still. These experiences might have left us struggling to believe that anything good could happen. So we are bewildered and fearful of even worse horrors. So many of us are mired in the anxiety that freezes over us and closes down movement and growth. We worry about bad things happening to those we love, and exist in a half-life of dread.

But the young man in white says: 'Do not be alarmed' – just as similar heavenly visitors had reassured Mary, and then the shepherds at Jesus' birth: 'Do not be afraid' (Luke 1:30; 2:10). This builds on a tradition throughout the Old Testament, such as when God speaks in Isaiah 43:1: 'Do not fear, for I have redeemed you; I have called you by name, you are mine.'

This offers a pattern by which God leads us from fear to rejoicing in his love, and basking in the light of his infinite grace towards us. God has bought us back, redeemed us – and not in a vague or haphazard way; but with an approach that is specific to each one of us. He has called us by our name. We are utterly his. So he has met us in the details of our fears; grappled with them, head on; and called us to belong to him, and to become the person whom he created us to be.

Father, draw me through the terrors of the night,
towards the light of your grace.

RACHEL BOULDING

An attitude of gratitude

O give thanks to the Lord, for he is good; his steadfast love endures for ever! Let Israel say, 'His steadfast love endures for ever'... The Lord is my strength and my might; he has become my salvation.

These verses are among the readings set by churches for Easter Day. They celebrate God's triumph over enemies, specifically death. But it is important that the psalm begins not in any sense of supremacy, but in what matters most: God's steadfast love.

In only 16 words, the first sentence sets up all that we ever need to know: God loves us, and bears us up with this love; he is utterly good; and we can respond to this wonder by thanking him. Such thanks are not a perfunctory 'Ta', but a whole approach to life. As the old saying has it: it's an attitude of gratitude. If we realise that life is a marvellous gift, for which we can be profoundly thankful, the most basic stuff is transformed.

It is God who has given us all this. He 'is my strength and my might' (v. 14). As a result, 'he has become my salvation'. In this view, God did not start off as my salvation, but his actions and my recognition of them have enabled him to become this.

All this is far more than a simple statement: instead, it is an action by God, a positive offer, made in generous love. I can respond to it with thankful acceptance and a desire to be saved. If all this sounds a bit high-flown, it need not be. Each day, I can try going about my God-given life with a sense of thankfulness for what I have, rather than for what I have not got. I happen to have probably only a year ahead of me, but I have already been given 52 great years. Many people get less than that, in worldly terms at least, but God's time is different, and way beyond our comprehension: 'With the Lord one day is like a thousand years, and a thousand years are like one day' (2 Peter 3:8).

Father, thank you for your overflowing gifts of life. Work in me to relish your amazing grace, in whatever time that I have now.

RACHEL BOULDING

'The readiness is all'

I shall not die, but I shall live, and recount the deeds of the Lord. The Lord has punished me severely, but he did not give me over to death... I thank you that you have answered me and have become my salvation... This is the Lord's doing; it is marvellous in our eyes. This is the day that the Lord has made; let us rejoice and be glad in it.

When I first read these verses, I laughed at the irony of my situation of having a diagnosis of terminal cancer. I may be still alive now, but not for much longer. There is a sense in which I have been given 'over to death' already (v. 18). But, gallows humour aside, isn't that the whole point? All of us are going to die. As Hamlet says in Shakespeare's play, speaking of death: 'If it be now, 'tis not to come. If it be not to come, it will be now. If it be not now, yet it will come – the readiness is all.'

Since being told that I will die soonish, I have been struck by how much the notion of trying to prepare for death ought not to be reserved for the gravely ill or very old people. We should all be getting ready: it is where we are all heading.

But I really do not mean going about morbidly, grimly expecting the end at any moment – or even becoming so heavenly minded that I am of no earthly use. What I am getting at is something that I hope is healthier and more realistic. If we all had a more secure, grounded idea about the fact that we are going to die, we would be able to see our life more honestly. We could appreciate God's gift of this precious time. This is the day that he has made, so we can be glad in it (v. 24). Such an approach focuses only on this world, and so is not the whole picture (as we shall see later), but it is a vital part of our Christian vision, and one that we all need to face.

Father, lead me to a clear-eyed sense of my present and future, savouring the days you have made.

RACHEL BOULDING

The grace of God that is with me

Now I should remind you, brothers and sisters, of the good news that I proclaimed to you, which you in turn received, in which also you stand, through which also you are being saved… But by the grace of God I am what I am, and his grace towards me has not been in vain. On the contrary, I worked harder than any of them – though it was not I, but the grace of God that is with me.

These verses are among those set for reading in church on Easter Day, while most of the rest of the chapter is the traditional passage for funerals. Yet so many people – even decent Christians – struggle to take in its message. Paul tells us that God loves us and has poured out his grace on us, giving victory over death – and yet we cannot cope with all this. Perhaps this should not be too surprising, as God's infinite generosity is far beyond anything we can imagine. Our limited human brain and heart cannot grasp God's utter goodness and endless love, as we are so often mired in our grudging tit-for-tat ideas about the good and bad that we think we and other people deserve. But God gives us life anyway. We can only respond with a feeble reflection, loving 'because he first loved us' (1 John 4:19).

Even our attempts to earn God's favour do not fit the picture: they look pretty pathetic alongside the way that God has given us everything. As Paul says in verse 11: 'I worked harder… though it was not I, but the grace of God that is with me.' It is God's work that is inside us. It is hardly even accurate to pray: 'Lord, help me to do decent things,' because it is not really me who is doing good – instead, it is God within me who does the business. A more truthful prayer would be: 'Lord, work in me to bring about your good purposes.' I can open myself more to God's will, but my own efforts are not what get things done.

Then Mary said, 'Here am I, the servant of the Lord; let it be with me according to your word' (Luke 1:38).

RACHEL BOULDING

Alive to God

But now is Christ risen from the dead, and become the firstfruits of them that slept. For since by man came death, by man came also the resurrection of the dead. For as in Adam all die, even so in Christ shall all be made alive.

This is the basis of our hope for our future life with God. We know that, in the ordinary course of things, we will all die after our limited span, and in human terms, that is the end of it: in Adam all die. But that is really not the final episode of our story. We will be made alive in Christ. We live in him now – we abide in him – and we will also live in him in the future, in a different and impossible-to-imagine way. 'Your life is hidden with Christ in God' (Colossians 3:3). We are bound up in his love, now and for ever. This is the love that cannot be destroyed by death: it carries on beyond the end of our life on earth, and is taken up to God. Those who remain still love those who have gone.

So how can we grasp this now, in our everyday experience? I am wary of the 'pie in the sky when you die' approach, which is such a distortion of Christian faith. Part of our response to God now, in living an Easter life, is surely to build on yesterday's verses about God's grace working in us.

We can be like Mary: we can say yes to God – although we can also say no, and many of us spend much energy trying to hide from him. But if we do say yes, then it is God who does the work in us. Mary did not make herself pregnant: she let God overshadow her, so that he could form the child inside her. In a similar way, God can form Jesus in us, if we allow him to. As we sing at Christmas in 'O little town of Bethlehem': 'Be born in us today.' So God works with and within us, and we live in him.

'We know that Christ, being raised from the dead, will never die again; death no longer has dominion over him' (Romans 6:9).

RACHEL BOULDING

God's love is untouched by death

For the love of Christ urges us on, because we are convinced that one has died for all; therefore all have died. And he died for all, so that those who live might live no longer for themselves, but for him who died and was raised for them... So if anyone is in Christ, there is a new creation: everything old has passed away; see, everything has become new!

This Easter week, we have moved from death to new life – life that God has given us to enjoy now, in its abundance, to bask in his love and share his gifts with our fellow creatures. This is our purpose.

We have also seen that, when this life ends, God has given us a sure hope for the future. It is not a distraction from the tasks of this life, or (God forbid) a smug secret that we have an exclusive, future haven, but an inspiration to spread God's love now, wherever we can.

For the moment, we live between the griefs of this world – although they can be shot through with glimpses of God's glory – and the certainty that our life here will end. In an Easter sermon in 2008 when he was Archbishop of Canterbury, Rowan Williams drew this out beautifully. 'When death happens and growing stops... there is only God left... We shall die, we shall have no choice but to let go of all we cling to, but God remains. God's unshakeable love is untouched by death, and all we do and all we care about matters to him.'

We all need to face that death is the end of everything we have known. We will leave this world naked, with nothing of our own remaining. But death does not destroy God, so we are each left with him – not hoping for survival, but for recreation in him.

I don't find it particularly helpful to speculate on the details of heaven, but I have been given a sense that I will be with God when I die. I will be taken care of, in God's loving embrace. He will be there, and I will be held secure in his new creation.

'In Christ shall all be made alive' (1 Corinthians 15:22, KJV).

* The sermon I mention is published in Rowan Williams, *Choose Life* (Bloomsbury, 2013).

RACHEL BOULDING

God's blessings

God's blessings abound – in creation, people, the Bible. Often we don't notice how he's blessing us, however, and we can miss out on fostering a thankful heart. I hope that as we work through a snapshot of some of God's blessings in this fortnight of Bible readings, your eyes will be opened afresh to his wonders around us.

We'll start at creation in Genesis, for when God made humanity and the animals, he blessed them and told them to thrive. We'll trace the story of his blessings on his people, the Israelites, and how he set them apart by leading them to a new land, though they often turned from him. We'll explore blessings as beatitudes, not only in the Psalms but in Jesus' famous Sermon on the Mount. We'll also look at some of the blessings written in the letters of the apostles before we end with the promises in Revelation.

In the Old Testament, often the Lord gave blessings that resulted in the people receiving physical blessings; of food and land, for instance. In the New Testament, in contrast, the blessings are usually more spiritual in nature, including the promise of everlasting life. How God blesses us is fully up to him – we can't demand how he will answer our requests. Nor should we interpret the lack of physical blessings as him not answering our prayer. He is God and we are not – but we can trust that he loves us and hears us.

Another caution to note concerns a so-called 'prosperity gospel' interpretation of blessings. We'll find a corrective to this theology when we reach some of the New Testament readings towards the end of our time together, for we'll see how God can bless us when we face trials.

I hope you will come away from this examination of our gracious, giving Lord with a renewed sense of awe and thanksgiving. For supremely the Lord sent his Son to die for us, and after Jesus' resurrection he sent his Spirit to dwell in us. We are no longer alone, for we have the presence of God with us day by day – surely the biggest blessing we'll ever receive.

AMY BOUCHER PYE

Created and blessed

Then God said, 'Let us make mankind in our image, in our likeness, so that they may rule over the fish in the sea and the birds in the sky, over the livestock and all the wild animals, and over all the creatures that move along the ground.' So God created mankind in his own image, in the image of God he created them; male and female he created them. God blessed them and said to them, 'Be fruitful and increase in number; fill the earth and subdue it. Rule over the fish in the sea and the birds in the sky and over every living creature that moves on the ground.'

The story of God's blessings starts right at the beginning, when he created the world with its creatures and the people he made in his image. The first instance of his blessings in the Hebrew scriptures comes in Genesis 1:22 when he blessed the living things, and here he extends it to men and women. These words of his favour continue throughout the Pentateuch, the first five books of the Bible.

What may appear to be a command in verse 28 of filling the earth and ruling over the creatures actually forms part of God's blessing, and not only for Adam and Eve, but also for their descendants. Note too the implication that the Lord wants a relationship with his people, for he speaks to them when blessing them.

As we live after the fall of humanity, and we witness the things that go wrong in the world and in our hearts, we may be tempted to discount the story of creation and the love that underpins it. After all, we see and experience pain, destruction and injustice. But when we consider the story from the point of view of God's original intentions, we can remember not only his goodness but how he entrusts us, who are made in his image, to create and to order our lives.

The world may not be as God made it originally, but he yet blesses us and wants us to flourish.

Lord God, show me today how I can be creative and fruitful.

AMY BOUCHER PYE

A call and a blessing

The Lord had said to Abram, 'Go from your country, your people and your father's household to the land I will show you. I will make you into a great nation, and I will bless you; I will make your name great, and you will be a blessing. I will bless those who bless you, and whoever curses you I will curse; and all peoples on earth will be blessed through you.' So Abram went, as the Lord had told him.

The Lord called Abraham (here 'Abram', before the Lord changed his name) so that he could bless him. He wanted to make him into a 'great nation' (v. 2) with many descendants, but for Abraham to receive these blessings he had to obey the Lord. The call involved leaving behind not only Abraham's country but his people – his inheritance and his family duties. The ancient Near East valued families strongly, so Abraham would have felt the weight of this call.

Abraham didn't vacillate, however, but obeyed God immediately as he packed up himself, his family and his possessions and embarked on the journey to the land of Canaan. Although he was 75 years old, he set out on this new adventure, trusting that God would fulfil his promises. He embraced the blessings in advance as he became a stranger and a foreigner; in the words of the writer to the Hebrews: 'He was looking forward to the city with foundations, whose architect and builder is God' (Hebrews 11:10).

Although God may not call us on the grand level that he did with Abraham, he still calls us to be his people. Part of this includes obedience, that we would heed his commands. We may have to leave our people, as Abraham did, or perhaps we may have to commit to staying in our home town or village. When we hear God and obey, we can trust that he too will bless us – whatever he decides that blessing will be.

Consider when you've felt God's call in your life. How much cost was involved? Did you sense God's blessing?

AMY BOUCHER PYE

Unearned blessings

When Israel saw the sons of Joseph, he asked, 'Who are these?' 'They are the sons God has given me here,' Joseph said to his father. Then Israel said, 'Bring them to me so I may bless them.'... Then he blessed Joseph and said, 'May the God before whom my fathers Abraham and Isaac walked faithfully, the God who has been my shepherd all my life to this day, the Angel who has delivered me from all harm – may he bless these boys. May they be called by my name and the names of my fathers Abraham and Isaac, and may they increase greatly on the earth.'

Many times in the Old Testament we see a father blessing his sons before he dies – Abraham, Isaac and Jacob all blessed their sons, and here Jacob blesses his grandsons. But the blessing that they bestow often isn't what the recipients may have expected. Namely, the younger son becomes the heir rather than the elder son, as happened with Jacob and Esau when Jacob tricked Isaac into giving him his blessing (Genesis 27:1–40). But in this story (and you might want to read the full account in Genesis 48), Jacob knowingly blesses the younger grandson, even though Joseph objected and tried to get him to change his mind.

This story reminds us that God is the fount of blessings, and that we can't demand, expect or shift his gifts. We may think that we all should receive an equal portion out of the cup of his blessings, but as the recipients we don't have the right to dictate the actions of the giver. We may know this truth intellectually, but we may harbour a sense of injustice deep within when we approach God.

One antidote to feeling like we're living with an attitude of scarcity is to list the things for which we're grateful. Doing so will train us to notice something that we might otherwise have overlooked – the smile of a stranger, the beauty of a flower, having clean water – and may infuse our hearts with gratitude and joy.

Father God, you bestow blessings on me daily. Give me eyes to see them,
and a grateful heart to receive them.

AMY BOUCHER PYE

Threefold blessing

The Lord said to Moses, 'Tell Aaron and his sons, "This is how you are to bless the Israelites. Say to them: 'The Lord bless you and keep you; the Lord make his face shine on you and be gracious to you; the Lord turn his face towards you and give you peace.'" So they will put my name on the Israelites, and I will bless them.'

One of the most famous passages in the Hebrew Bible is this blessing that Moses instructed Aaron and his sons to pray – with Aaron signifying the Israelite priests. Its threefold format has suggested to some Christians that it foreshadows the Trinity, that is, God the Father, Son and Holy Spirit. Indeed, this blessing is often known as the 'three-in-one' blessing.

The Lord wanted his people to receive his blessing, and so he instructed his priests how to extend it. The first clause, that the Lord would 'bless you and keep you', reminded the people that they were God's chosen and loved ones who would know his protection. The second clause, that the Lord would 'make his face to shine on you and be gracious to you', could have brought to mind Moses' experience when he met with the Lord up the mountain and received the book of the law, and descended with his face aglow. Similarly, the Lord wants to meet with his people. And the third clause, that the Lord would 'turn his face towards you and give you peace', is the climax of the prayer. The Hebrew word for 'peace' is *shalom*, which is not just the absence of conflict but the fullness of life and a state of well-being. And this is what the Lord wants to give his loved ones. The blessing concludes with the Lord putting his very name on his people – they will be known to and by him.

The priests in the temple would use this prayer of blessing as a bene-diction, and today the practice continues in many churches – and in many homes as a night-time practice. Binding these words on our hearts will help us to embrace them as the gift that they are.

Lord, may I receive your blessings, and may I pass them along to others.

AMY BOUCHER PYE

Choose life!

See, I set before you today life and prosperity, death and destruction. For I command you today to love the Lord your God, to walk in obedience to him, and to keep his commands, decrees and laws; then you will live and increase, and the Lord your God will bless you in the land you are entering to possess… This day I call the heavens and the earth as witnesses against you that I have set before you life and death, blessings and curses. Now choose life, so that you and your children may live and that you may love the Lord your God, listen to his voice, and hold fast to him. For the Lord is your life, and he will give you many years in the land he swore to give to your fathers, Abraham, Isaac and Jacob.

As Moses reached the end of his life, he knew he would not be entering the promised land with the Israelites. After blessing the twelve tribes, he made a final summary and clarion call for God's people to live well and to choose life. Theirs is the choice – choose disobedience by worshipping other gods, which will lead to destruction, or choose life by walking in the way of the Lord, which will lead to blessings and peace. As the Israelites had wandered in the desert for 40 years, hearing about a land of milk and honey (see Exodus 3:8) must have encouraged them to follow the Lord.

'Now choose life' – and life not only for them, but for their children. The Lord holds this out as the fulfilment of his promise, a great blessing. Indeed, he fulfilled this promise through sending his Son Jesus to earth as the Messiah. And Jesus is the life; he said, 'I am the resurrection and the life. The one who believes in me will live, even though they die' (John 11:25). When we choose to follow Jesus, we receive life and his light, and no longer need to fear the darkness.

Consider how you can choose life today, and what path you might follow.

Lord Jesus Christ, you are the way, the truth and the life.
We come to the Father through you (see John 14:6).

AMY BOUCHER PYE

The path of life

Blessed is the one who does not walk in step with the wicked or stand in the way that sinners take or sit in the company of mockers, but whose delight is in the law of the Lord, and who meditates on his law day and night. That person is like a tree planted by streams of water, which yields its fruit in season and whose leaf does not wither – whatever they do prospers. Not so the wicked! They are like chaff that the wind blows away.

Psalm 1 paints a picture of a life of contrasts. On the one hand is the person who follows God, who delights in his law and ruminates on it. On the other hand is the wicked; they are without depth and weight, and fly away in the breeze like chaff. As we think of this contrast, it's worth digging into the original language to understand the meaning. When we read the word 'blessing', we may think of the meaning associated with the Hebrew word *baruk*, which signifies the blessings that God bestows on individuals and groups, such as we've seen earlier this week. But here, the psalmist uses the Hebrew word *'ashar* for blessed, which has the meaning of a beatitude – it's a statement that commends the way a person lives. Thus this psalm is a statement about how to flourish through which path to take.

We might find the contrast difficult, for the psalmist etches no middle ground. A person is either blessed or wicked, with the gifts and consequences that follow. It may be that this psalm was used in teaching the young, conveying a sense of urgency through the contrasting views of how one lives one's life.

We can be responsible only for the path we choose to walk. If we're tempted to veer off to the wide and broad 'road that leads to destruction' (see Matthew 7:13), we can ask for God's help to return to his way of holiness and goodness. May our lives be those that yield their fruit in season (v. 3).

Father God, may we delight in your law and meditate on it with joy.
In it we find the way to life and flourishing.

AMY BOUCHER PYE

Seek wisdom

Blessed are those who find wisdom, those who gain understanding, for she is more profitable than silver and yields better returns than gold. She is more precious than rubies; nothing you desire can compare with her. Long life is in her right hand; in her left hand are riches and honour. Her ways are pleasant ways, and all her paths are peace. She is a tree of life to those who take hold of her; those who hold her fast will be blessed.

A key to well-being and contentment in life – to being blessed – according to the aptly named wisdom literature that we see in the book of Proverbs, is to seek and attain wisdom. We may think that we need wealth to be happy, but the author of the Proverbs points to wisdom as being more profitable than precious metals or jewels. Those who abound in wisdom will enjoy lives of peace – which again is the Hebrew word that implies well-being, *shalom*.

Note in verse 13 how the verbs 'find' and 'gain' imply an intentional search for wisdom; it's something to be desired and sought after. Similarly, once wisdom is found, people are to 'hold fast' to it (v. 18). Some will work to refine silver or gold, or to polish up precious stones, but even more should they seek God's wisdom. For this will lead to 'pleasant ways' and 'peace' – to being blessed.

We too can ask the Lord for wisdom, and trust that he will honour our request. We may find that we grow in knowledge and understanding as we study the Bible, talk with other Christians and wait before God in prayer. Of course, we can also study the world in all of its riches and intricacies to gain wisdom and understanding. Why not commit to setting aside some time each week for study? An increasing number of online courses are available, as well as free lectures. May we put wisdom as 'an ornament to grace [our] neck' (Proverbs 3:22).

Consider a time when you reached a new insight or understanding.
What was your process of coming to that knowledge?
How can you pursue wisdom?

AMY BOUCHER PYE

Blessed are...

Blessed are the poor in spirit, for theirs is the kingdom of heaven. Blessed are those who mourn, for they will be comforted. Blessed are the meek, for they will inherit the earth. Blessed are those who hunger and thirst for righteousness, for they will be filled. Blessed are the merciful, for they will be shown mercy. Blessed are the pure in heart, for they will see God. Blessed are the peacemakers, for they will be called children of God. Blessed are those who are persecuted because of righteousness, for theirs is the kingdom of heaven. Blessed are you when people insult you, persecute you and falsely say all kinds of evil against you because of me.

We read the beatitudes in Psalm 1 about the blessed person; here Jesus preaches what has become the most famous sermon ever, known as the Sermon on the Mount, in which he starts with his list of beatitudes. Blessed, he says, are those who are the opposite of what the world praises. Rather, blessed are those who mourn, who hunger and thirst, who are merciful, who are pure in heart. Blessed are the peacemakers and the persecuted; blessed are the insulted. In short, blessed are those who stand against the cultural tides and who follow the Lord, for they will find God's kingdom.

In an age when convenience and prosperity seem to be the prized cultural values in the developed world, Jesus' words can startle us when we slow down and think about them. For those who have been Christians for many years, these words will be familiar – almost too familiar for us to notice how radical they are. But when was the last time you felt blessed when you were insulted for your faith? I can't remember when I felt persecuted for my beliefs.

Today, perhaps you could make the time to ponder Jesus' words. You could write them out and consider what it would mean to be poor in spirit, or meek, or merciful. Even embracing just one of the beatitudes could have a transforming effect on our lives.

Lord Jesus Christ, you saw the outcasts and the ones who were discarded in society. Open my eyes to see all those whom you love.

AMY BOUCHER PYE

The blessed king

The next day the great crowd that had come for the festival heard that Jesus was on his way to Jerusalem. They took palm branches and went out to meet him, shouting, 'Hosanna!' 'Blessed is he who comes in the name of the Lord!' 'Blessed is the king of Israel!' Jesus found a young donkey and sat upon it, as it is written: 'Do not be afraid, Daughter Zion; see, your king is coming, seated on a donkey's colt.' At first his disciples did not understand all this. Only after Jesus was glorified did they realise that these things had been written about him…

The crowds assembled in Jerusalem to celebrate the Passover feast, swelling the city to twice its size. They greeted Jesus with requests for help and shouts of blessing: 'Hosanna!' which means 'Save us now!' and was a cry of the Psalms (118:25), and 'Blessed is he who comes in the name of the Lord!' which appeared in the same psalm (118:26). But the crowds also added a nationalistic cry, 'Blessed is the king of Israel!' – which is not what Jesus intended.

Jesus rode into Jerusalem on a humble donkey, signifying that he was not a war-hero king who would rule with force. The crowds, increasingly whipping themselves into a frenzy, wished otherwise. Even the disciples, those who had spent so much time with Jesus, misunderstood. Only after his death did they put the pieces together to comprehend the kind of king he was.

As we see in this story, words of blessing may be spoken inappropriately. The pilgrims to Jerusalem who shouted to Jesus were looking for a national messiah to save them from the Romans. But what they got, if they would receive him, was a Saviour who came in peace and who ushered in a new kingdom of grace and truth.

If you have a palm cross from Palm Sunday a few weeks ago, why not use it as a prayer aid today? If you tip it on its side, it appears to be a sword. If you stand it up straight, it becomes a cross.

Lord Jesus Christ, you came humbly on a donkey to usher in
a new kingdom. May I welcome you as king.

AMY BOUCHER PYE

Blessing, not cursing

Love must be sincere. Hate what is evil; cling to what is good. Be devoted to one another in love. Honour one another above yourselves. Never be lacking in zeal, but keep your spiritual fervour, serving the Lord. Be joyful in hope, patient in affliction, faithful in prayer. Share with the Lord's people who are in need. Practise hospitality. Bless those who persecute you; bless and do not curse. Rejoice with those who rejoice; mourn with those who mourn. Live in harmony with one another. Do not be proud, but be willing to associate with people of low position. Do not be conceited.

As we read this section of Paul's letter to the Romans, we might think that it feels like a burst of staccato statements that don't relate to each other. But biblical commentators say he's following an ancient practice called paranesis, which combines wisdom and common teachings into a group of short statements that quickly move from one topic to the next. Paul's readers would have been familiar with this style, understanding that he's combining wisdom into a series of imperatives for them to follow.

In verse 14, Paul echoes Jesus' Sermon on the Mount when he says, 'Bless those who persecute you' (see Matthew 5:10–11). Here he's probably speaking of those outside the church community, as he moves between giving advice on how to treat fellow Christians and advice for those who do not share their beliefs. Paul follows Jesus' countercultural teaching of not to retaliate when one is cursed, but to bless one's enemy.

What a different world we'd live in if everyone embraced this way of life. Instead of wars escalating on an international scale, peace would be achieved more easily. The division of families, with siblings not speaking to each other for years, could be avoided. Even the way people drove their cars could be changed radically – probably with fewer road accidents.

May the Lord give us the gift of blessing others when we're wronged, and may we receive and embrace the grace of this gift.

Lord Jesus Christ, you reveal how to live according to your kingdom, and not according to the world. Fill me with your presence that I might share your love.

AMY BOUCHER PYE

The gift of giving

'Now I commit you to God and to the word of his grace, which can build you up and give you an inheritance among all those who are sanctified. I have not coveted anyone's silver or gold or clothing. You yourselves know that these hands of mine have supplied my own needs and the needs of my companions. In everything I did, I showed you that by this kind of hard work we must help the weak, remembering the words the Lord Jesus himself said: "It is more blessed to give than to receive."' When Paul had finished speaking, he knelt down with all of them and prayed.

The apostle Paul is saying goodbye to the leaders in the church at Ephesus, expecting never to see them again. Therefore, his words hold an extra weight, as he tries to impress on them the necessity of sacrifice for others. He says how he supported himself in his ministry, probably in comparison to the travelling teachers of the time who would teach in the expectation of being paid. Paul wants to stress the integrity with which he has come, and bids the leaders to live similarly.

And then we come to the comment that fits with our theme of blessing, which Paul says Jesus said: 'It is more blessed to give than receive' (v. 35). Although this saying isn't recorded in the Gospels, we know that much of what Jesus did and said isn't captured there. Paul speaks of a surprising truth, which seems backwards to what the world would say – that we receive more joy and blessing through giving than receiving.

This is a somewhat trivial example, but those who love giving gifts know this to be true. The sheer pleasure of finding just the right item to express one's knowledge of the other person's likes and desire surpasses the experience of receiving a gift. How much more this is true when we give of ourselves in the Lord's service.

Today and this week, why not look for ways to give to someone? Remember it doesn't have to be something material.

Lord Jesus Christ, shape me and mould me, that I might reflect your glory and give to others from your riches.

AMY BOUCHER PYE

Persevering through trials

Consider it pure joy, my brothers and sisters, whenever you face trials of many kinds, because you know that the testing of your faith produces perseverance. Let perseverance finish its work so that you may be mature and complete, not lacking anything. If any of you lacks wisdom, you should ask God, who gives generously to all without finding fault, and it will be given to you... Blessed is the one who perseveres under trial because, having stood the test, that person will receive the crown of life that the Lord has promised to those who love him.

'Bless you, prison, for having been in my life!' People were amazed to hear Aleksandr Solzhenitsyn make this remark, as one who spent eleven years in the forced labour camps in the former Soviet Union. But he writes in *The Gulag Archipelago* (1958–68) how, there in prison, he realised the difference between good and evil. He also understood his own capacity for evil, which was the opposite of what he thought when he entered the gulag. Therefore, he saw the blessing of that time of trial.

The blessings that we have seen in the Old Testament were sometimes connected with prosperity, which can make modern commentators link these promises to a gospel of prosperity. But by doing so, they miss out on the truth that Solzhenitsyn hints at – the blessing we receive by persevering through trials. As we live in a fallen world, we won't find our lives to be without the blemish of disappointment, sin and disease. We will all encounter trials at some point, and when we do, we can look to the Lord for the strength to persevere. In these moments, prayer is key, as we see in verse 5, for the Lord will grant us wisdom when we ask.

Think about any 'prisons' you may have been trapped in, and how you found release. If this is the case, now when you look back, are you able to say with Solzhenitsyn, 'Bless you, prison'?

Lord of all mercy, give me resilience, that I can stand when I face the storms in my life. Teach me to look to you for help and encouragement, and may I be one who perseveres.

AMY BOUCHER PYE

Repaying evil with blessings

Finally, all of you, be like-minded, be sympathetic, love one another, be compassionate and humble. Do not repay evil with evil or insult with insult. On the contrary, repay evil with blessing, because to this you were called so that you may inherit a blessing. For, 'Whoever would love life and see good days must keep their tongue from evil and their lips from deceitful speech. They must turn from evil and do good; they must seek peace and pursue it. For the eyes of the Lord are on the righteous and his ears are attentive to their prayer, but the face of the Lord is against those who do evil.'

A so-called 'natural' response when we are treated abysmally is to lash out. We've been hurt, and we want to hurt the perpetrator in return. But repaying evil for evil sets off a seemingly never-ending cycle of destruction and bitterness. The disciple Peter was aware of this when he wrote to believers scattered around the provinces of Rome, those who were experiencing deep persecution. He knew they were being abused for their beliefs, but he wanted them not to mimic their persecutors.

One of the most difficult things must be to 'repay evil with blessing', but stories of forgiveness abound in this 'unnatural' act. The stories of outlandish grace stand out because they seem so hard to believe, such as that of Terri Roberts, the mother of a man who gunned down 15 Amish girls in the States in 2006. This mother reached out to the Amish families, asking them to forgive her son, and a strong new friendship resulted. This is a striking example, but everyday stories can be seen and experienced in our communities, when old rivals forgive each other and seek to do good, or siblings come together in harmony after years of strife.

Repaying evil with blessings might not be the first thing we want to do when wronged, but when we bring the matter before God, he can give us the strength to forgive.

Lord God, bring unity to our churches, helping us to love each other and to put the needs of others above our own.

AMY BOUCHER PYE

A blessed feast

'Let us rejoice and be glad and give him glory! For the wedding of the Lamb has come, and his bride has made herself ready. Fine linen, bright and clean, was given her to wear.' (Fine linen stands for the righteous acts of God's holy people.) Then the angel said to me, 'Write this: Blessed are those who are invited to the wedding supper of the Lamb!' And he added, 'These are the true words of God.'

As we come to the end of our exploration of God's blessings, it seems fitting to reflect on Revelation, with its apocryphal vision of things to come. For although Jesus has ushered in God's new kingdom on earth, we who love and follow him will experience the blessings unending that await us in the life to come.

Note how the 'blessed' in verse 9 indicates a beatitude, as we have seen previously. By this, John, the writer of Revelation, means that those who are invited to the celebration should persevere through difficult and testing times.

The Lord has spoken of the wedding supper previously in the Hebrew scriptures, when the prophet Isaiah said, 'On this mountain the Lord Almighty will prepare a feast of rich food for all peoples, a banquet of aged wine – the best of meats and the finest of wines' (Isaiah 25:6). It's a celebration he doesn't want his children to miss.

I've been pondering how I can have an attitude of celebration and jubilee when I feel tired, overwrought or stretched to the limits. One discipline I'm practising is to pause and be present in the moment – to listen to my husband or children when they speak, for instance. Another practice I'm working on is to give thanks each day. My attitude shifts to wonder and gratitude when I notice the beauty around me.

Thank you for travelling this journey! May the Lord God bless you and keep you; may he make his face to shine upon you and be gracious to you, and give you his peace.

Lord God, you invite us to the best feast ever and clothe us with white linen. May we accept your invitation and look forward with joy.

AMY BOUCHER PYE

Songs of praise

I sometimes hear the comment that we shouldn't have favourite passages of scripture because the Bible is inspired and therefore to be loved in its entirety. Thank goodness that isn't true for hymns! I know many of you will have your own favourites – perhaps from your wedding day or a special occasion or simply because, as you sing it still, it allows you to worship God with freedom and joy. I can recall singing my own favourite hymn for the first time and wondering how on earth the author captured such wonderful truth about Jesus, his death and resurrection. I still sing that hymn with gusto, although less tunefully than once I managed! You can read about it in this series of meditations.

Of course, the wonder of hymns is that they enable us to say particular things about God or each other: they articulate faith in the face of hardship and even death; they tell us about Jesus and his life, death and resurrection. Sometimes they ask deep questions which cannot always be answered, and sometimes they stir us and send us out with renewed confidence to live for the Lord. What is important is that they invite us to engage with God, to receive and respond to him with faith and action.

This series is called 'Songs of praise' and tries to marry some of my favourite hymns with passages from the Bible so they stand together. In this way, the hymns pick up on scripture and allow the Bible and, more importantly, faith in the Lord of scripture, to be expressed in a context of worship. Essentially, I think hymn singing is a way of saying something when words alone will not suffice. The music allows the words to come alive, and worship and devotion to flow. I hope you will think about the hymns that have shaped your own life and faith and which still nurture your walk with God. I pray that this selection will resonate with you and inspire you to think, pray and worship the Lord God with new love and devotion.

ANDREW JOHN

Praise to the Lord

Sing to the Lord a new song; sing to the Lord, all the earth. Sing to the Lord, praise his name; proclaim his salvation day after day. Declare his glory among the nations, his marvellous deeds among all peoples. For great is the Lord and most worthy of praise; he is to be feared above all gods. For all the gods of the nations are idols, but the Lord made the heavens. Splendour and majesty are before him; strength and glory are in his sanctuary. Ascribe to the Lord, all you families of nations, ascribe to the Lord glory and strength.

My childhood upbringing was in a fairly religious home, although my Sunday ambition usually extended no further than attempting to avoid churchgoing. I became a master of devising all kinds of excuses, even how to appear so ruddy that the only possible explanation was a severe fever (rather than holding my breath under the pillow for as long as I could manage). For me, worship was utterly boring and meaningless.

So when I came to faith and discovered the joy of singing praises to God, it exploded everything I had thought about Christianity and even God! To discover that this act was the very thing we were made to offer was a revelation. To discover God, no longer contained in musty old books, but as a living Lord full of endless energy and love, transformed my life. I remain profoundly grateful today for that moment of recognition. The words below are an invitation to come and discover the wonder of God in worship; to realise that the Lord of all is worthy of our deepest and most joyful praise. We were created to worship and to enjoy God. Worship stands at the heart of Christian faith and holds our energies and attention in a Godward direction. Whatever else today may bring let there be glad adoration, for God the Unchanging is worthy of praise.

Praise to the Lord, the Almighty, the King of creation! O my soul, praise him, for he is thy health and salvation! All ye who hear, now to his temple draw near; praise him in glad adoration ('Praise to the Lord, the Almighty', Joachim Neander, 1680).

ANDREW JOHN

Love eternal free and boundless

He is before all things, and in him all things hold together. And he is the head of the body, the church; he is the beginning and the firstborn from among the dead, so that in everything he might have the supremacy. For God was pleased to have all his fullness dwell in him, and through him to reconcile to himself all things, whether things on earth or things in heaven, by making peace through his blood, shed on the cross. Once you were alienated from God and were enemies in your minds because of your evil behaviour. But now he has reconciled you by Christ's physical body through death to present you holy in his sight, without blemish and free from accusation.

I can remember the first time I climbed Snowdon. It was a bright and beautiful day without a cloud in the sky (an unusual event!). When we reached the summit, England and Wales lay before us and the scene was astonishing in its scale and grandeur. Seeing the 'big picture' not only emphasised how small I was, but how vast the world was – even this tiny part of it. This is important for Christians because it gives perspective and should cause us to worship the Lord with awe and wonder.

The words from this hymn are my favourite because that is what they do: they tell us that God is the author of all creation whose power sustains everything. However, here it isn't just vastness of creation, but the remarkable wonder of God's salvation in Jesus. These words tell us of God's plan, before the creation of the world, to provide a saviour who would save us from sin and whose name is greater than any other. That is the measure of his wondrous love for humanity and the extent of his grace and care. Today, remember that God prepared for your forgiveness before the foundation of the world.

Ere he raised the lofty mountains, formed the seas or built the skies, love eternal, free and boundless, moved the Lord of life to die, foreordained the prince of princes for the throne of Calvary ('Come ye faithful raise the anthem', John Mason Neale, 1863).

ANDREW JOHN

His mercy is forever

Who shall separate us from the love of Christ? Shall trouble or hardship or persecution or famine or nakedness or danger or sword? As it is written: 'For your sake we face death all day long; we are considered as sheep to be slaughtered.' No, in all these things we are more than conquerors through him who loved us. For I am convinced that neither death nor life, neither angels nor demons, neither the present nor the future, nor any powers, neither height nor depth, nor anything else in all creation, will be able to separate us from the love of God that is in Christ Jesus our Lord.

I had no idea what my friends meant when they kept harping on about Romans. In fact, no one had told me that the Bible could be read, let alone that it could contain life-changing truth. So when I heard Paul expound his vision and certain hope in these few verses, it was like letting the light flood into a darkened room, the door of which had been long shut.

Paul's confidence is that Christ's saving death has such power that it keeps us safe even beyond the chill waters of death. He does not explain in great detail how he thinks this relates to that Christian command to persevere (but he is clear there is such a mandate), yet this does not lessen the strong and unbreakable confidence he has in the grace and power of the cross. It is this which provides the foundation for our lives and our resolve to follow him faithfully and obediently; it is this which holds us fast when we might otherwise fail. The verses below, from an Easter hymn, capture that same confidence. Jesus' death marked a journey in which he passed on ahead of us, depriving death of its power over us and securing our place in heaven. This too gives us confidence that nothing, not even death, can part us from God.

Death's waters lost their chill when Jesus crossed the river.
His love shall reach me still; his mercy is forever
('This joyful Eastertide', George R. Woodward, 1894).

ANDREW JOHN

Ours the cross, the grave, the skies

Love never fails. But where there are prophecies, they will cease; where there are tongues, they will be stilled; where there is knowledge, it will pass away. For we know in part and we prophesy in part, but when completeness comes, what is in part disappears. When I was a child, I talked like a child, I thought like a child, I reasoned like a child. When I became a man, I put the ways of childhood behind me. For now we see only a reflection as in a mirror; then we shall see face to face. Now I know in part; then I shall know fully, even as I am fully known. And now these three remain: faith, hope and love. But the greatest of these is love.

These verses come from a chapter in the Bible which is perhaps one of, if not *the* most famous of all in scripture. This so-called 'Hymn to Love' features in weddings consistently because its poetry and power are unsurpassed. But the verses I have chosen describe the consequences of love in the light of the relationship we will one day enjoy with God. We shall see him, in the language of an older Bible, not as 'through a glass darkly' (KJV) but, here in the NIV, 'face to face'.

Paul has no doubt that one day we shall be with the Lord and know God fully. That is an extraordinary thought – to know God fully! So much of our earthly life is marked by an awareness of our mortal limitations – we may know the Lord well and yet miss a guiding hand or prompting from above; we may pray often and with real fervour yet see prayers go unanswered; and we may long for holiness and yet fail and fall. One day it will not be so. The verses below from a great Easter hymn point in that very direction. In Christ, we are crucified, in Christ we die to sin and in Christ we shall be presented holy and spotless before our loving heavenly Father.

Soar we now where Christ has led, following our exalted Head;
made like him, like him we rise, ours the cross, the grave, the skies
('Love's redeeming work', Charles Wesley, 1739).

ANDREW JOHN

All my trust

'But if, in seeking to be justified in Christ, we Jews find ourselves also among the sinners, doesn't that mean that Christ promotes sin? Absolutely not! If I rebuild what I destroyed, then I really would be a law-breaker. For through the law I died to the law so that I might live for God. I have been crucified with Christ and I no longer live, but Christ lives in me. The life I now live in the body, I live by faith in the Son of God, who loved me and gave himself for me. I do not set aside the grace of God, for if righteousness could be gained through the law, Christ died for nothing!'

The conversation was to the point. I had been told in no uncertain terms to be quiet! 'Religion is a private matter,' the person said, and I was to stop pressing him on what he thought faith meant. I've thought about that conversation many times since, and still think faith must be always personal but never private.

Paul speaks about his own faith in the verses above; the Christ he followed loved him and gave himself for him. It is a moving testimony to the wonder of a personal relationship. Paul's faith was not a matter of following rules (although the law of love was very important). Neither was it a lifestyle choice or worldview. It was from beginning to end about Christ, knowing him and the power of his resurrection (Philippians 3:10). The verses below are taken from the second verse of 'Jesus lover of my soul'. The tune 'Aberystwyth' is often used because the gravity of the words suit the minor key. The words are also deeply personal; there is a cleaving to God, a resting on his secure and steady help which will not fail. Today, make this same resting on God your experience and prayer.

Other refuge have I none, hangs my helpless soul on thee; leave, ah! leave me not alone, still support and comfort me! All my trust on thee is stayed; all my help from thee I bring; cover my defenceless head with the shadow of thy wing ('Jesus lover of my soul', Charles Wesley, 1740).

ANDREW JOHN

It is well

That day when evening came, he said to his disciples, 'Let us go over to the other side.' Leaving the crowd behind, they took him along, just as he was, in the boat. There were also other boats with him. A furious squall came up, and the waves broke over the boat, so that it was nearly swamped. Jesus was in the stern, sleeping on a cushion. The disciples woke him and said to him, 'Teacher, don't you care if we drown?' He got up, rebuked the wind and said to the waves, 'Quiet! Be still!' Then the wind died down and it was completely calm. He said to his disciples, 'Why are you so afraid? Do you still have no faith?' They were terrified and asked each other, 'Who is this? Even the wind and the waves obey him!'

When we come to believe in Christ, it can seem that a whole new world has been opened to us and we will never have a care again. That kind of illusion quickly evaporates when reality bites! The truth is that each of us will face countless challenges in our walk with God and these may involve family or employment or issues of mobility and health.

I have been moved by those who face ongoing difficulties and whose faith yet sustains them. Wounds can threaten to scar and debilitate, and the cost can be considerable. However, it is this which often becomes a source of blessing in a way that I do not fully understand. We experience something of Christ through such people and their hardships. I think such people show us the truth of the lines penned below. They speak of loss, but also of how Christ is a comfort, bringing peace and hope when we might otherwise despair. I pray you may find this same thing should you feel overwhelmed and when icy waters threaten to overwhelm you. Hear Jesus say 'Be still.'

When peace like a river attendeth my way, when sorrows like sea billows roll; whatever my lot, thou hast taught me to say, 'It is well, it is well with my soul' ('When peace like a river', Horatio Spafford, 1876).

ANDREW JOHN

Slow tears

When one of the Pharisees invited Jesus to have dinner with him, he went to the Pharisee's house and reclined at the table. A woman in that town who lived a sinful life learned that Jesus was eating at the Pharisee's house, so she came there with an alabaster jar of perfume. As she stood behind him at his feet weeping, she began to wet his feet with her tears. Then she wiped them with her hair, kissed them and poured perfume on them. When the Pharisee who had invited him saw this, he said to himself, 'If this man were a prophet, he would know who is touching him and what kind of woman she is – that she is a sinner.'

Few stories in the New Testament are as beautiful as the one recorded above. We see an act of love and devotion pitted against a hard and brittle attachment to righteous living, devoid of compassion or mercy. At the heart of the good news we see Jesus reaching out to those who feel despair and are utterly lost, and lifting them up, loving them and forgiving them in restoring grace.

The beautiful words below are from a hymn written many years ago by a priest of the Church of England called Phineas Fletcher. He captures the unadulterated joy of forgiveness and the tears which follow. Tears like this cannot be manufactured nor are they the sort which come from regret over something wasted or lost. It may not be very British to express this kind of emotion, but I have come to believe that tears like this are a gift, and flow when the darkness and brokenness of our lives are laid bare before God without excuse or caveat.

When honesty characterises our life in God, we walk in the light and are formed into people who, knowing their own frailties, can show compassion and grace to others. Joy and tears can sit together in a life of openness and lead us to that depth of love for God, the very thing for which our souls cry out.

Drop, drop, slow tears, and bathe those beauteous feet, which brought from Heav'n the news and Prince of Peace ('Drop, drop, slow tears,' Phineas Fletcher, 1633).

ANDREW JOHN

Through all the changing scenes

Even if I should choose to boast, I would not be a fool, because I would be speaking the truth. But I refrain, so no one will think more of me than is warranted by what I do or say, or because of these surpassingly great revelations. Therefore, in order to keep me from becoming conceited, I was given a thorn in my flesh, a messenger of Satan, to torment me. Three times I pleaded with the Lord to take it away from me. But he said to me, 'My grace is sufficient for you, for my power is made perfect in weakness.' Therefore I will boast all the more gladly about my weaknesses, so that Christ's power may rest on me. That is why, for Christ's sake, I delight in weaknesses, in insults, in hardships, in persecutions, in difficulties. For when I am weak, then I am strong.

We do not know what this 'thorn in the flesh' was for Paul. Some have argued it was a difficult companion. Others have suggested it was an ongoing condition like epilepsy, something debilitating which would accompany Paul throughout his days.

It is not important we know what it was, but rather we should focus on how the apostle responded to it. In the spirit of another great hymn, he took it 'to the Lord in prayer'. This act takes us beyond a faith which will only accept good things and to a depth of grace in which we can find God at the very heart of difficulties and pain. This does not explain why such hardships come about, of course, but provides a way of coping and responding faithfully. Paul's experience is all the more extraordinary because he came to see that what God had sent was something which made him more faithful, more dependent upon God. The hymn below conveys that same faith. It acknowledges there will be trials but that finding God in the midst of them leads to deeper praise and stronger love.

Through all the changing scenes of life, in trouble and in joy, the praises of my God shall still my heart and tongue employ ('Through all the changing scenes of life', Nahum Tate and Nicholas Brady, 1696).

ANDREW JOHN

I cannot tell

Then Jesus came to them and said, 'All authority in heaven and on earth has been given to me. Therefore go and make disciples of all nations, baptising them in the name of the Father and of the Son and of the Holy Spirit, and teaching them to obey everything I have commanded you. And surely, I am with you always, to the very end of the age.'

I remember seeing my son dive 20 feet into a deep pool when on holiday. That he somersaulted too made it more heart-stopping than ever! However, what I remember most was the look of delight on his face as he launched forth. This was something he had looked forward to and wasn't going to be denied.

That spirit of adventure gets us to the heart of the passage above. Jesus commissions his disciples to go and live the gospel and to make it known to everyone. This is no fearful or paralysing command (although it is sometimes understood or experienced in this way) but a call to tell good news. When a needy world hears there is hope and a life of purpose and joy to sustain it, it is a transforming moment. No wonder Jesus told stunning stories of heaven rejoicing when one person believed (Luke 15:7).

We do not need to be perfect to be bearers of hope and those who have a story of grace to share. We simply need our story and confidence in Jesus. The words below provide the inspiration for our task. They anticipate the completion of that Great Commission, but firmly root success in the grace and power of God. It's this which makes sharing faith a joy and privilege.

I cannot tell how he will win the nations, how he will claim his earthly heritage, how satisfy the needs and aspirations of east and west, of sinner and of sage. But this I know, all flesh shall see his glory, and he shall reap the harvest he has sown, and some glad day his sun shall shine in splendour when he the Saviour, Saviour of the world, is known
('I cannot tell', William Fullerton, 1929).

ANDREW JOHN

Reading *New Daylight* in a group

SALLY WELCH

I am aware that although some of you cherish the moments of quiet during the day that enable you to read and reflect on the passages we offer you in *New Daylight*, other readers prefer to study in small groups, to enable conversation and discussion and the sharing of insights. With this in mind, here are some ideas for discussion starters within a study group. Some of the questions are generic and can be applied to any set of contributions within this issue; others are specific to certain sets of readings. I hope they generate some interesting reflections and conversations!

General discussion starters

These questions can be used for any study series within this issue. Remember, there are no right or wrong answers; they are intended simply to enable a group to engage in conversation.

- What do you think the main idea or theme of the author is in this series? Do you think they succeeded in communicating this to you, or were you more interested in the side issues?

- Have you had any experience of the issues that are raised in the study? How have they affected your life?

- What evidence does the author use to support their ideas? Do they use personal observations and experience, facts, quotations from other authorities? Which appeals to you most?

- Does the author make a 'call to action'? Is that call realistic and achievable? Do you think their ideas will work in the secular world?

- Can you identify specific passages that struck you personally – as interesting, profound, difficult to understand or illuminating?

- Did you learn something new reading this series? Will you think differently about some things, and if so, what are they?

Crowds (Sally Welch)

Thinking about all the different crowds encountered in the Gospel stories, which ones would have been particularly exciting? And which would have felt most threatening?

Have you ever witnessed the power of a crowd? Was it for good or evil? Have you ever joined in with a crowd, such as at a political demonstration or a musical event? How did this feel?

Blessings (Amy Boucher Pye)

Amy writes about repaying 'evil with blessings' (1 Peter 3:9). How easy do you think this might be? Have you ever tried to do this and what has been the result? How do you manage to find blessings through the challenging times of your life and has this helped you to cope?

Reflective question (Blessings, Amy Boucher Pye)

Psalm 1 commends those who walk in the path of the Lord. What helps you to do this? What challenges do you face as you try and 'delight' in God's word?

Delight in the Lord!

Author profile: Liz Hoare

How long have you been an Anglican priest, and what first inspired you to seek ordination?

I was ordained deacon in 1989 and was among the first women to be ordained priest in 1994, in Durham Cathedral. I was inspired partly by meeting women who were training for ministry in the Church of England, partly through the wise counsel of an older Christian friend and partly through my own research into the sixteenth-century church and the difference made by women who took God's call on their life seriously.

Your biography says that you teach 'spiritual formation'. What does that entail?

Spiritual formation is about forming Christian character. It comes about by cooperating with the Holy Spirit and by putting in place practices to help us live lives that are a natural expression of Jesus' life and teachings.

How do you think a theological college differs from a secular training institution?

A theological college is a community of people learning theology and the practical skills needed to lead churches. Many communities in Oxford study, eat and socialise together, but a theological college also prays together and seeks the development of character as well as minds and practical skills.

How did you get involved with writing for *New Daylight* and how are you finding the experience of writing Bible study notes?

I was asked to write for *New Daylight* after talking to the editor about the value of providing guidance on reading the Bible. I enjoy the challenge of imagining how the chosen book or theme could help people in their walk with God and I find that putting the daily readings together helps me personally as well.

Which spiritual writers have influenced you and in what ways?

Different writers have been important at different times in my life. I read a lot of C.S. Lewis as a young adult. Later I began reading spiritual classics, such as St Augustine's *Confessions* and keep going back to these. I love Eugene Peterson's writing because he writes as a Bible teacher and also as a pastor. And I love the Christian poets: R.S. Thomas, Gerard Manley Hopkins, Malcolm Guite and Denise Levertov, for example.

What are your New Year's resolutions for 2018?
To make more time for friendships that matter.

Recommended reading

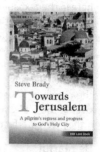

BRF's 2018 Lent book is by Steve Brady. *Towards Jerusalem* is a unique Lent book, a call to live for a vision bigger than ourselves, marching to a different drumbeat towards 'Zion', God's New Jerusalem, and all that this means for today's Christian. The following extracts are two of the readings.

A place for tears

Read Genesis 23:1–4 and 16–20.

'Death has climbed in through our windows and has entered our fortresses' is the graphic way the prophet Jeremiah describes the one great certainty of life (Jeremiah 9:21). Whether it comes through the windows, doors or sewers into the dwelling of our lives, arrive it will. Its statistics are most impressive, according to a quip by George Bernard Shaw: 'one out of one people die'. As I am writing this, I am trying to contact a relative whose husband woke up fighting for breath during the night and was gone before the ambulance arrived. Every day in every generation, the great drama predicted back in Genesis is played out, 'dying you shall die' (2:17, literal translation).

Abraham may be on his way to his perceived promised land but his life's partner, Sarah, will not be there to enjoy it with him. Here's a lesser-known city we'll all visit sooner or later, Kiriath Arba. And some of us today are still red-raw with grief after visiting there with a loved one whom we had to leave behind, whether yesterday or years ago. Grief has many guises and disguises, and is as long as a piece of string. It is shortened or lengthened by many factors. How do we cope when Kiriath Arba beckons? May Abraham's example, with a few additions to it, turn us to the God who 'heals the broken-hearted and binds up their wounds' (Psalm 147:3).

Be thankful

What a life Sarah and Abraham had shared. Indeed, the Hebrew idiom here in the text speaks about the '*lives* of Sarah' (v. 1). I suspect when you have lived to 127 that's one way to put it! She had set out with Abram on a journey of faith (Genesis 11:31), and had almost ended up not once but twice in some potentate's harem (12:14–20; 20:1–18). Then, at 90, she'd given birth to a son (21:1–7). Like any life, it was not perfect, for neither was she. Her advice that Abram should sleep with her maid, Hagar, and the cruelty it subsequently provoked (16:1–16; 21:8–21) are not glossed over in the Bible. We are wise not to canonise in death our loved ones, as if they were perfect, even though they were wonderful to us.

Be tearful

One of the positive elements to have entered our funeral culture in recent years is the note of celebration, the opportunity to be grateful for a loved one's life. What is concerning to some of us who conduct such events is that the bereaved are almost discouraged from grieving at all. We emphasise the departed's accomplishments, we smile at their foibles and we send them off with a blast of Frank Sinatra's version of 'My Way'. In contrast, Abraham 'went to mourn for Sarah and to weep over her' (v. 2).

This was not because he had no hope, or did not know about some form of life after death. Rather, as Paul reminds the Thessalonians, it was okay to grieve, but not 'like the rest of mankind, who have no hope' (1 Thessalonians 4:13). After all, at the death of Lazarus, the Lord Jesus himself wept (John 11:35). But why the grief if we 'go to heaven when we die'? Because the Bible views death as an unlawful intruder who robs us of life. It is still 'the last enemy' (1 Corinthians 15:26), though it is not the last word – Christ is! Tears are important in the grief process.

Be resourceful

In death, there is a great deal to be done by the living, as this chapter amply demonstrates. Abraham needs to negotiate with Ephron the Hittite for a burial site. The oriental customs involved, alien to many of us, of bargaining over the price, discreetly mentioned, may mean Abraham paid 'over the odds' (vv. 10–16). On the other hand, we are acting wisely when we prepare in life for what we wish for in death. It has been my privilege to carry out, sometimes scrupulously, the wishes of the departed in terms of hymns chosen, things to say, passages to read – and people to avoid! Thoughtful planning, clear communication, and the valuing of the opportunity that one's funeral may present are to be commended.

Be hopeful

It would be a mistake to leave this chapter concluding that it is an ancient version of how to pre-plan a funeral. Let's notice that the passage is topped and tailed by an electrifying word in its context, Canaan (vv. 2, 19). This is what Abraham's journeying is about. Although he is 'a foreigner and stranger' (v. 4), he now has a foothold and a grave in the promised land!

It is not, to be sure, the holy city, but it is a marker on the way, even in death, of the promise of life. In laying Sarah's remains to rest Abraham, in a way yet to be explained, is anticipating the fulfilment of the promise of the one who says, 'a time is coming and has now come when the dead will hear the voice of the Son of God and those who hear will live', even those in the grave (John 5:25, 28). Christians are to face death, acknowledging both its pain and horror, while thanking God for Jesus, the resurrection and the life!

A dying thief, a living hope

Read Luke 23:38–43.

'These verses… deserve to be printed in letters of gold. They have probably been the salvation of myriads of souls,' commented the great J.C. Ryle, the first Anglican bishop of my hometown of Liverpool. But not everyone, for here are three men: one died *in* sin; another *to* sin; the third *for* sin.

It is often assumed when people are in deep straits, especially approaching the end of life, that a 'just in case there is a God' insurance-policy faith kicks in. But pain, suffering and certain death do not necessarily lead to a death-bed conversion, as the first criminal's behaviour highlights. Like the rulers who 'sneered' (v. 35) and the soldiers who 'mocked' (v. 36), this man 'hurled insults' at Jesus (v. 39). Terrifyingly, he illustrates that it is possible to be near to Jesus, speak to Jesus and die with Jesus, and yet be lost. Someone wisely remarked that the essence of heaven is to say to God, 'Your will be done', while the essence of hell is when God says to us, 'Your will be done!' This man was a successful rebel to the end.

In stark contrast, there hangs another thief. Both Matthew and Mark record that both criminals 'heaped insults' on Jesus (Matthew 27:44; Mark 15:32). So what changed his attitude to Christ? Commentators have speculated that he had heard Jesus preach. Others, that he knew that both Pilate and Herod thought Jesus innocent. Yet others, that his conscience was pricked by our Lord's prayer for his enemies and his calm demeanour in death. Who knows? What is clear, however, is that he feared God, owning up to his wrongdoing (vv. 40–41). He believed, despite the evidence to the contrary, that Jesus did have a kingdom (as the title on Jesus's cross inadvertently advertised), and he wanted to be part of it (vv. 38, 42). He had no good works to offer, no possibility of enjoying the sacraments, no church to join. But he repented, believed and was saved. Amazing grace!

And why is Jesus there, between two criminals (v. 33)? A thief too? He fed the five thousand. A murderer? He healed the sick and raised the dead. The victim of a miscarriage of justice? Undoubtedly, but he said he could call on 'twelve legions of angels' to deliver him (Matthew 26:53). So why is he there? Two charges emerge from the gospel records: blasphemy (Mark 14:64) and rebellion (Luke 23:14). The irony here is that the centurion confesses that Jesus is both 'a righteous man' and 'the Son of God' (Luke 23:47; Mark 15:39).

Truly, he had 'done nothing to deserve death' (Luke 23:15). We have! Don't we all stand as rebels before a holy God? Aren't there times when we feel the lure of almightiness, the blasphemy that we are kings of the castle, godlike creatures on earth without a God up there to whom we are accountable? The gospel comes to tell us of one who has taken the hit for our pride and folly. If the released felon Barabbas, 'thrown into prison for insurrection and murder' (23:25), had turned up at the cross, he might accurately have said, 'That man is there in my place, paying my price, dying my death, so I can go free!' But only Barabbas? Truly, 'We all, like sheep, have gone astray… and the Lord has laid on him the iniquity of us all'; for 'the Son of Man… [came] to serve, and give his life a ransom for many' (Isaiah 53:6; Mark 10:45).

A church I visited years ago had a sermon in stone on an outside wall. It consisted of three crosses, the one on the left pointing inwards towards the central cross and the one on the right pointing away. Wisely, Bishop Ryle reminds us: 'One thief was saved that no sinner might despair; but only one, that no sinner might presume.' Which way am I looking as the Lord of glory gives his life as a ransom for the world?

To order a copy of this book, please turn to the order form on page 149.

Recommended reading

Called by God

Exploring our identity in Christ

DEREK TIDBALL
pb, 978 0 85746 530 6 £7.99

Who am I? It's a question many of us ask ourselves at some point in life. In this fascinating book, Derek Tidball explores finding who God is calling us to be and what he is calling us to do. He explores twelve key New Testament texts which speak of the Christian's calling. In a time when we can get lost in the quest for identity, this book brings us back to the Bible and to Christ at the centre of it all.

The Recovery of Joy

Finding the path from rootlessness to returning home

NAOMI STARKEY
pb, 978 0 85746 518 4 £6.99

Naomi Starkey weaves imaginative stories with profound biblical reflections on several of the psalms to trace a journey that many of us will relate to. The narrative begins in rootlessness and despair, and takes the reader across the sea to a series of islands. These are the settings for a sequence of events and encounters through which we can progress from that initial rootlessness, through healing, to a rediscovery of the joy of feeling at the centre of God's loving purpose for our lives.

Engaging the Word

Biblical literacy and Christian discipleship

PETER M. PHILLIPS
pb, 978 0 85746 583 2 £7.99

Peter Phillips is convinced that the church in the West is not devouring the Bible; it's not meditating on the word as it should. *Engaging the Word* will transform the Bible engagement habits of Christian disciples and leaders. It will make an impact on the spiritual health of the church – opening new opportunities for drawing on God's word and new life as a result. A series of practical explorations of the role of the Bible will help readers reach up to God, reach in to develop understanding of identity in Christ and to reach out to others.

Jesus through the Old Testament

Transform your Bible understanding

GRAEME GOLDSWORTHY
pb, 978 0 85746 567 2 £7.99

Confident in the Old Testament?

Enjoying reading it?

Happy to preach from it?

In this engaging book, Graeme Goldsworthy reflects with clarity and practical insight on reading and using the Old Testament. By showing us how Jesus is central to the Old Testament's message, he encourages us to reinstate it as essential and transformative to our lives, churches and mission in today's world. The author asks important questions: Where is Jesus in the whole biblical storyline? How does the kingdom of God relate to him? In what way is he central to the divine revelation? This is a must-read for those who wish to transform their biblical understanding.

Living the Prayer
The everyday challenge of the Lord's Prayer

TRYSTAN OWAIN HUGHES
pb, 978 0 85746 623 5 £7.99

Living the Prayer is a fresh perspective on the Lord's Prayer. Rooted in the Bible as well as in contemporary culture, it explores how this prayer can radically challenge and transform our daily lives. Contained in the prayer's seventy words is a fresh and innovative way of viewing, and acting in, the world that is as relevant now as it was 2,000 years ago. The author shows that this revolutionary prayer demands that we don't remain on our knees, but, rather, that we work towards making God's topsy-turvy, downside-up kingdom an everyday reality.

To order

Online: brfonline.org.uk
Telephone: +44 (0)1865 319700
Mon–Fri 9.15–17.30

Delivery times within the UK are normally
15 working days. Prices are correct at the time of
going to press but may change without prior notice.

BRF

Title	Price	Qty	Total
Towards Jerusalem	£7.99		
Called by God	£7.99		
The Recovery of Joy	£6.99		
Engaging the Word	£7.99		
Jesus through the Old Testament	£7.99		
Living the Prayer	£7.99		
Seasoned by Seasons	£7.99		

POSTAGE AND PACKING CHARGES			
Order value	UK	Europe	Rest of world
Under £7.00	£2.00	£5.00	£7.00
£7.00–£29.99	£3.00	£9.00	£15.00
£30.00 and over	FREE	£9.00 + 15% of order value	£15.00 + 20% of order value

Total value of books	
Postage and packing	
Total for this order	

Please complete in BLOCK CAPITALS

Title .... First name/initials .... Surname...

Address...

....Postcode...........................

Acc. No. .... Telephone ....

Email...

Please keep me informed about BRF's books and resources ❏ by email ❏ by post
Please keep me informed about the wider work of BRF ❏ by email ❏ by post

Method of payment

❏ Cheque (made payable to BRF)   ❏ MasterCard / Visa

Card no. ☐☐☐☐ ☐☐☐☐ ☐☐☐☐ ☐☐☐☐ ☐☐☐☐ ☐☐☐☐

Valid from ☐☐ ☐☐   Expires ☐☐ ☐☐   Security code* ☐☐☐

Last 3 digits on the reverse of the card

Signature* .... Date .... /.......... /..........

*ESSENTIAL IN ORDER TO PROCESS YOUR ORDER

Please return this form to: BRF, 15 The Chambers, Vineyard, Abingdon OX14 3FE | enquiries@brf.org.uk
To read our terms and find out about cancelling your order, please visit **brfonline.org.uk/terms**.

The Bible Reading Fellowship (BRF) is a Registered Charity (233280)

How to encourage Bible reading in your church

BRF has been helping individuals connect with the Bible for over 90 years. We want to support churches as they seek to encourage church members into regular Bible reading.

Order a Bible reading resources pack

This pack is designed to give your church the tools to publicise our Bible reading notes. It includes:

- Sample Bible reading notes for your congregation to try.
- Publicity resources, including a poster.
- A church magazine feature about Bible reading notes.

The pack is free, but we welcome a £5 donation to cover the cost of postage. If you require a pack to be sent outside the UK or require a specific number of sample Bible reading notes, please contact us for postage costs. More information about what the current pack contains is available on our website.

How to order and find out more

- Visit **biblereadingnotes.org.uk/for-churches**
- Telephone BRF on +44 (0)1865 319700 Mon–Fri 9.15–17.30
- Write to us at BRF, 15 The Chambers, Vineyard, Abingdon OX14 3FE

Keep informed about our latest initiatives

We are continuing to develop resources to help churches encourage people into regular Bible reading, wherever they are on their journey. Join our email list at **biblereadingnotes.org.uk/helpingchurches** to stay informed about the latest initiatives that your church could benefit from.

Introduce a friend to our notes

We can send information about our notes and current prices for you to pass on. Please contact us.

Transforming lives and communities

BRF is a charity that is passionate about making a difference through the Christian faith. We want to see lives and communities transformed through our creative programmes and resources for individuals, churches and schools. We are doing this by resourcing:

- **Christian growth and understanding of the Bible.** Through our Bible reading notes, books, digital resources, Quiet Days and other events, we're resourcing individuals, groups and leaders in churches for their own spiritual journey and for their ministry.

- **Church outreach in the local community.** BRF is the home of three programmes that churches are embracing to great effect as they seek to engage with their local communities: Messy Church, Who Let The Dads Out? and The Gift of Years.

- **Teaching Christianity in primary schools.** Our Barnabas in Schools team is working with primary-aged children and their teachers, enabling them to explore Christianity creatively and confidently within the school curriculum.

- **Children's and family ministry.** Through our Parenting for Faith programme, websites and published resources, we're working with churches and families, enabling children and adults alike to explore Christianity creatively and bring the Bible alive.

Do you share our vision?

Sales of our books and Bible reading notes cover the cost of producing them. However, our other programmes are funded primarily by donations, grants and legacies. If you share our vision, would you help us to transform even more lives and communities? Your prayers and financial support are vital for the work that we do.

- You could support BRF's ministry with a one-off gift or regular donation (using the response form on page 153).
- You could consider making a bequest to BRF in your will (page 152).
- You could encourage your church to support BRF as part of your church's giving to home mission – perhaps focusing on a specific area of our ministry, or a particular member of our Barnabas in Schools team.
- Most important of all, you could support BRF with your prayers.

Make a lasting difference through a gift in your will

BRF's story began in 1922 when a vicar in Brixton, south London, introduced daily Bible readings to help his congregation 'get a move on spiritually'. Over the coming years, several other churches joined the scheme and more and more copies of the Bible reading notes were printed. By 1939 an amazing 238,000 copies were being printed and read.

The past 90 years have certainly seen BRF flourish. We still produce and distribute Bible reading notes, but our work now encompasses so much more and its impact stretches across the globe, from Brixton to Brisbane.

Today we are the home of creative programmes like Messy Church, which reaches an estimated 500,000 people each month. We encourage churches to reach out to fathers through Who Let The Dads Out? and we help meet the spiritual needs of older people through The Gift of Years. We also enable primary schools to teach Christianity creatively within the curriculum, and equip parents to effectively disciple their children through Parenting for Faith. At the heart of it all is a desire to help children and adults of all ages explore Christianity and grow in faith.

If you share our passion for making a difference through the Christian faith, please consider leaving a gift in your will to BRF. Gifts in wills are an important source of income for us and they don't need to be huge to make a real difference. For every £1 we receive we invest 95p back into charitable activities. Just imagine what we could do over the next century with your help.

For further information about making a gift to BRF in your will, please visit **brf.org.uk/lastingdifference**, contact Sophie Aldred on **01865 319700** or email **giving@brf.org.uk**.

Whatever you can do or give, we thank you for your support.

SHARING OUR VISION – MAKING A GIFT

I would like to make a gift to support BRF. Please use my gift for:

☐ where it is needed most ☐ Barnabas Children's Ministry
☐ Messy Church ☐ Who Let The Dads Out? ☐ The Gift of Years

Title	First name/initials	Surname

Address		
		Postcode

Email

Telephone

Signature	Date

gift aid it You can add an extra 25p to every £1 you give.

Please treat as Gift Aid donations all qualifying gifts of money made

☐ today, ☐ in the past four years, ☐ and in the future.

I am a UK taxpayer and understand that if I pay less Income Tax and/or Capital Gains Tax in the current tax year than the amount of Gift Aid claimed on all my donations, it is my responsibility to pay any difference.

☐ My donation does not qualify for Gift Aid.

Please notify BRF if you want to cancel this Gift Aid declaration, change your name or home address, or no longer pay sufficient tax on your income and/or capital gains.

Please complete other side of form ➡

Please return this form to:
BRF, 15 The Chambers, Vineyard, Abingdon OX14 3FE

The Bible Reading Fellowship is a Registered Charity (233280)

SHARING OUR VISION – MAKING A GIFT

Regular giving

By Direct Debit:

☐ I would like to make a regular gift of £ ⬚ per month/quarter/year.
Please also complete the Direct Debit instruction on page 159.

By Standing Order:

Please contact Priscilla Kew +44 (0)1235 462305 | giving@brf.org.uk

One-off donation

Please accept my gift of:

☐ £10 ☐ £50 ☐ £100 Other £ ⬚

by (delete as appropriate):

☐ Cheque/Charity Voucher payable to 'BRF'

☐ MasterCard/Visa/Debit card/Charity card

Name on card ⬚

Card no. ⬚⬚⬚⬚ ⬚⬚⬚⬚ ⬚⬚⬚⬚ ⬚⬚⬚⬚

Valid from ⬚M⬚M⬚Y⬚Y Expires ⬚M⬚M⬚Y⬚Y

Security code* ⬚⬚⬚ *Last 3 digits on the reverse of the card
ESSENTIAL IN ORDER TO PROCESS YOUR PAYMENT

Signature ⬚ Date ⬚

We like to acknowledge all donations. However, if you do not wish to receive an acknowledgement, please tick here ☐

↩ Please complete other side of form

Please return this form to:
BRF, 15 The Chambers, Vineyard, Abingdon OX14 3FE

The Bible Reading Fellowship is a Registered Charity (233280)

ND0118

NEW DAYLIGHT SUBSCRIPTION RATES

Please note our new subscription rates, current until 30 April 2019:

Individual subscriptions
covering 3 issues for under 5 copies, payable in advance
(including postage & packing):

	UK	Europe	Rest of world
New Daylight	£16.95	£25.20	£29.10
New Daylight 3-year subscription (9 issues) (not available for Deluxe)	£46.35	N/A	N/A
New Daylight Deluxe per set of 3 issues p.a.	£21.45	£32.25	£38.25

Group subscriptions
covering 3 issues for 5 copies or more, sent to **one** UK address (post free):

New Daylight	£13.50 per set of 3 issues p.a.
New Daylight Deluxe	£17.25 per set of 3 issues p.a.

Please note that the annual billing period for group subscriptions runs from 1 May to 30 April.

Overseas group subscription rates
Available on request. Please email **enquiries@brf.org.uk**.

Copies may also be obtained from Christian bookshops:

New Daylight	£4.50 per copy
New Daylight Deluxe	£5.75 per copy

All our Bible reading notes can be ordered online by visiting
biblereadingnotes.org.uk/subscriptions

For information about our other Bible reading notes,
and apps for iPhone and iPod touch, visit
biblereadingnotes.org.uk

NEW DAYLIGHT INDIVIDUAL SUBSCRIPTION FORM

All our Bible reading notes can be ordered online by visiting
biblereadingnotes.org.uk/subscriptions

☐ I would like to take out a subscription:

Title .... First name/initials .... Surname ....

Address ....

.... Postcode ....

Telephone .... Email ....

Please send *New Daylight* beginning with the May 2018 / September 2018 / January 2019 issue (*delete as appropriate*):

(please tick box)	UK	Europe	Rest of world
New Daylight 1-year subscription	☐ £16.95	☐ £25.20	☐ £29.10
New Daylight 3-year subscription	☐ £46.35	N/A	N/A
New Daylight Deluxe	☐ £21.45	☐ £32.25	☐ £38.25

Total enclosed £ .... (cheques should be made payable to 'BRF')

Please charge my MasterCard / Visa ☐ Debit card ☐ with £ ....

Card no. ☐☐☐☐ ☐☐☐☐ ☐☐☐☐ ☐☐☐☐

Valid from ☐☐ ☐☐ Expires ☐☐ ☐☐ Security code* ☐☐☐

Last 3 digits on the reverse of the card

Signature* .... Date ...... /...... /......

*ESSENTIAL IN ORDER TO PROCESS YOUR PAYMENT

To set up a Direct Debit, please also complete the Direct Debit instruction on page 159 and return it to BRF with this form.

Please return this form with the appropriate payment to:
BRF, 15 The Chambers, Vineyard, Abingdon OX14 3FE

To read our terms and find out about cancelling your order, please visit **brfonline.org.uk/terms**.

The Bible Reading Fellowship is a Registered Charity (233280)

ND0118

NEW DAYLIGHT GIFT SUBSCRIPTION FORM

☐ I would like to give a gift subscription (please provide both names and addresses):

Title .... First name/initials .... Surname ....

Address ....

.... Postcode ....

Telephone .... Email ....

Gift subscription name ....

Gift subscription address ....

.... Postcode ....

Gift message (20 words max. or include your own gift card):

....

....

Please send *New Daylight* beginning with the May 2018 / September 2018 / January 2019 issue (*delete as appropriate*):

(please tick box)	UK	Europe	Rest of world
New Daylight 1-year subscription	☐ £16.95	☐ £25.20	☐ £29.10
New Daylight 3-year subscription	☐ £46.35	N/A	N/A
New Daylight Deluxe	☐ £21.45	☐ £32.25	☐ £38.25

Total enclosed £ .... (cheques should be made payable to 'BRF')

Please charge my MasterCard / Visa ☐ Debit card ☐ with £ ....

Card no. ☐☐☐☐ ☐☐☐☐ ☐☐☐☐ ☐☐☐☐

Valid from ☐☐ ☐☐ Expires ☐☐ ☐☐ Security code* ☐☐☐

Last 3 digits on the reverse of the card

Signature* .... Date ....../....../......

*ESSENTIAL IN ORDER TO PROCESS YOUR PAYMENT

To set up a Direct Debit, please also complete the Direct Debit instruction on page 159 and return it to BRF with this form.

Please return this form with the appropriate payment to:
BRF, 15 The Chambers, Vineyard, Abingdon OX14 3FE

To read our terms and find out about cancelling your order, please visit **brfonline.org.uk/terms**.

The Bible Reading Fellowship is a Registered Charity (233280)

DIRECT DEBIT PAYMENT

You can pay for your annual subscription to our Bible reading notes using Direct Debit. You need only give your bank details once, and the payment is made automatically every year until you cancel it. If you would like to pay by Direct Debit, please use the form opposite, entering your BRF account number under 'Reference number'.

You are fully covered by the Direct Debit Guarantee:

The Direct Debit Guarantee

- This Guarantee is offered by all banks and building societies that accept instructions to pay Direct Debits.

- If there are any changes to the amount, date or frequency of your Direct Debit, The Bible Reading Fellowship will notify you 10 working days in advance of your account being debited or as otherwise agreed. If you request The Bible Reading Fellowship to collect a payment, confirmation of the amount and date will be given to you at the time of the request.

- If an error is made in the payment of your Direct Debit, by The Bible Reading Fellowship or your bank or building society, you are entitled to a full and immediate refund of the amount paid from your bank or building society.

- If you receive a refund you are not entitled to, you must pay it back when The Bible Reading Fellowship asks you to.

- You can cancel a Direct Debit at any time by simply contacting your bank or building society. Written confirmation may be required. Please also notify us.

The Bible Reading Fellowship

Instruction to your bank or building society to pay by Direct Debit

Please fill in the whole form using a ballpoint pen and return it to:
BRF, 15 The Chambers, Vineyard, Abingdon OX14 3FE

Service User Number: | 5 | 5 | 8 | 2 | 2 | 9 |

Name and full postal address of your bank or building society

To: The Manager	Bank/Building Society
Address	
	Postcode

Name(s) of account holder(s)

Branch sort code

| | | – | | | – | | |

Bank/Building Society account number

| | | | | | | | | |

Reference number

| | | | | | | | |

Instruction to your Bank/Building Society
Please pay The Bible Reading Fellowship Direct Debits from the account detailed in this instruction, subject to the safeguards assured by the Direct Debit Guarantee. I understand that this instruction may remain with The Bible Reading Fellowship and, if so, details will be passed electronically to my bank/building society.

Signature(s)

Banks and Building Societies may not accept Direct Debit instructions for some types of account.

BRF

Transforming
lives and communities

Christian growth and understanding of the Bible

Resourcing individuals, groups and leaders in churches for their own
spiritual journey and for their ministry

Church outreach in the local community

Offering three programmes that churches are embracing
to great effect as they seek to engage
with their local communities
and transform lives

Teaching Christianity in primary schools

Working with children and teachers to explore Christianity creatively
and confidently

Children's and family ministry

Working with churches and families to explore Christianity creatively
and bring the Bible alive

Visit **brf.org.uk** for more information on BRF's work
Review this book on Twitter using **#BRFconnect**

brf.org.uk